OUT
A COURAGEOUS WOMAN'S
JOURNEY

OUT
A COURAGEOUS WOMAN'S JOURNEY

LOU ANNE SMOOT

SAPPHIRE BOOKS

SALINAS, CALIFORNIA

Editor - Shelley Thrasher
Book Design - LJ Reynolds
Cover Design - Michelle Brodeur

Sapphire Books Publishing, LLC
P.O. Box 8142
Salinas, CA 93912
www.sapphirebooks.com

Printed in the United States of America
First Edition – May 2016

This and other Sapphire Books titles can be found at
www.sapphirebooks.com

PREFACE

My dream of publicly sharing my story was first brought to fruition in 2013 by Sheri and Bob Adams and their Pair of Docs publishing. I was delighted when these theological educators, known for publishing "theology for the open hearted," excitedly latched on to my manuscript, which they released as A Christian Coming Out, A Journal of the Darkest Period in My Life. At that time, I believed the sharing of my painful past would persuade religious fundamentalists how irrational it is to believe that being gay is a choice. Much to my dismay, this target audience was not interested in my story.

Although I was personally able to sell quite a few copies of this book, I quickly realized my primary success lay in being a storyteller. By the end of December 2015, I had verbally shared my story with fifty-eight groups in multiple states. My most enthusiastic listeners were members of the gay community and their supporters.

(A video at https://vimeo.com/146166769 depicts my presentation.)

Our good friends Connie Ward and Shelley Thrasher envisioned that the LGBT community would embrace my story and shared their concept with Chris Svendsen, publisher of Sapphire Books Publishing, who agreed with them.

At their suggestion, I made three primary changes from my original book. First, I removed most of the scripture references; second, the story now flows along the same lines as my verbal presentation; and third, I have added many experiences, both church- and community-related, from my fifteen-year journey as an "out" LGBT advocate— some encouraging and heartwarming, some not so much.

In OUT: A Courageous Woman's Journey, I changed all but three names: mine, my wife Brenda's, and my daughter Laura's. I altered all other names to avoid any possible hurt or discomfort. My story, however, requires telling the truth in order for readers to understand my life journey, which at times has been very painful. If you recognize yourself in an incident you'd prefer to forget, I deeply apologize.

Dedication

Dedicated Posthumously To Marilyn Hillyer whose Christlike example led me safely through a very dark valley and helped me bear sorrow I thought I couldn't bear

With Thanks To Alice Parrish who started me on my journey through her words of love and acceptance and to Brenda McWilliams who supports me, encourages me, and loves me.

Acknowledgment

This book would not exist without the rhetoric of Marilyn Hillyer, known in this book as Barbara. This gifted writer passed away in 2006, and I continue to miss her so very much. The one I call Janie has blessed my life and remains my good friend and avid supporter.

I thank God every day for Brenda McWilliams, my wife, my friend, my supporter, my advisor, and my companion. We married on December 8, 2015 on the fifteenth anniversary of our covenant commitment to each other. I call her my special gift from God.

Many thanks to my four children, my brothers, and my sister-in-law for their love and support as I floundered in self-pity.

And a special thank you to Shelley Thrasher, my good friend and my very talented and skillful editor. Through her and her wife, Connie, the vision for this book emerged. I'm honored Shelley agreed to take on the job of editing my revised book and am so very thankful for her suggestions.

And a big thank you to all those at Sapphire Books Publishers

Chapter One

I was watching an old western on TV the summer of 2013, and toward the end of the movie, the hero said, "A man has to live with the hand he was dealt."

Immediately, I told myself, "That's what I'm doing now."

The hand I was dealt has me straddling the sometimes very deep divide between the gay community and the religious fundamentalist community.

Thank God, I've been able to maintain my balance in both communities for fifteen years.

❧ ❧ ❧ ❧

My story begins where most people's stories do, with parents. Mine were good people, hard-working and educated. My dad eventually retired as superintendent of schools in Little Rock, Arkansas, and my mother was a schoolteacher.

They were also Southern Baptist and brought me up in that religious tradition. My dad always served as a deacon, and both my parents taught adult Sunday-school classes. I took my religion so seriously, I even attended college at Baylor, the largest Baptist university in the world. And at Baylor I had to face the fact that I was different: my roommate and I fell desperately in love.

At thirteen or fourteen, I had strange feelings toward a particular girl in high school. One evening, six or seven of us girls were all squeezed together in a car, laughing and having a great time at a drive-in movie. I sat in the backseat, behind the driver and next to the door. Smashed next to me was Jean, a senior I admired. As a sophomore, I looked up to her as a role model. However, that night, aware of her close physical presence, I let shocking thoughts enter my mind. I wanted to kiss her. How wonderful that would be. I dismissed such a notion promptly. "How strange!" I told myself. "Why in the world am I thinking such things?"

My embarrassing desire confused and troubled me, and I never mentioned it to anyone, especially not Jean. I had to keep such unacceptable desires private. One other time, after an out-of-town football game, Jean and I sat beside each other on the school's band bus. During the long trip home that night, we were tired, it was late, and I was sleepy. Jean, always considerate, said, "Lou Anne, if you want to lie down and put your head in my lap, that's fine."

I did, and thought nothing of it, until Jean held my hand, probably so I wouldn't fall on the floor. Holding Jean's hand set my heart to hammering, and, ecstatic, I was immediately wide-awake. That was the most wondrous thing that had ever happened to me.

I never felt anything special toward any other girl until I fell in love with Karen, one of my roommates at Baylor. We were just innocent seventeen-year-olds.

Since I was from Big Spring, a small town in Texas, and she was from Chicago, neither of us knew anyone at Baylor or even Waco. So, when we first met, we were perhaps drawn toward each other because our other suite mates had friends at the school. We didn't.

We had a common need, a loneliness that the other filled—by talking.

The subject matter was immaterial. We discussed, we argued, we debated. We tossed our ideas and opinions back and forth. Hour after hour we shared our thoughts, our beliefs, our ideals, our hopes. If we agreed about an issue, one of us deliberately pretended to disagree just so we could have fun debating the subject. Never before had I found someone with whom I so enjoyed talking and sharing confidences. I suppose her intelligence first drew me to her.

Having no sisters, I'd never really confided in anyone. I'd always been one of the popular leaders in public school, but my conversations with my friends had never been deep, or thoughtful, or weighty. They were just typical teenage girly talk. Karen introduced me to a different type of conversation, and I thoroughly enjoyed it. Loved it.

An only child, she had been sheltered from the mainstream and grew up in an adult world. Her father was a professor of Old Testament at a Chicago seminary and had raised her as a strict member of the American Baptist church. Her friends, who were limited to students who attended her private school, lived in other parts of the city making it difficult for her to have much social interaction with them.

Our love of conversing instigated our physical relationship.

Baylor was very strict during the late '50s. As freshmen, we had to be in our rooms by eight thirty p.m. Monday through Thursday. We couldn't even visit with our suite mates next door after that deadline unless we "happened" to both be in the bathroom at the same time. (Six of us shared one small bath located between our rooms.) We had to turn out the lights by ten sharp, and hall monitors rigorously enforced these rules.

Karen and I would often be in the middle of a good discussion at ten o'clock. During our freshman year the dorms were so crowded that three girls shared a room designed for only two, with a bunk bed and a single bed. Three of us divided up space in two chest of drawers and two small closets.

Our third roommate was always ready to go to sleep by ten. Therefore, when the lights were turned off, and everyone was supposed to stop visiting, Karen and I climbed into one of our beds and whispered. We lay there, not touching, enjoying the opportunity to enter each other's minds and thoughts. Like an elixir to our need for companionship, our whispered conversations sometimes continued for hours.

After a few weeks, my longing to touch her, to just hold her hand, dominated my thoughts as we lay side by side talking. I ached with desire yet worried about doing something that might disgust her. Finally, I let my arm rest on the bed between us, next to hers but not touching. Did I dare hold her hand? Yes. A few minutes later, I gently clasped her hand. Neither of us mentioned what we were doing as we continued to whisper.

That was the start. From then on, whenever we continued talking in bed after lights out, we held hands. It was just understood. Neither of us ever said a word about it. Nothing changed in our relationship. We never touched each other at any other time—just held hands in bed. But before long, I ached for more and began to imagine what it would be like to kiss her.

One night, when our third roommate was gone for the weekend, Karen and I still climbed into the same bed to talk. That night we were on the top bunk, next to the hall door. We somehow went from hand-holding to cuddling. Then I propped myself up on my right elbow and leaned down and lightly, gently kissed Karen on the lips. She didn't seem displeased. She simply said, "I've never kissed a boy. How do you kiss?"

I'd dated regularly all through high school and had even gone steady my senior year, so she considered me an expert in this field. I explained, "Just part your lips slightly. You'll find it very natural."

She followed my instructions, and we kissed— lovingly and tenderly, then longingly, desperately, feverishly. That night we discovered a passion neither of us realized we possessed. After about an hour, Karen said, "We need to discuss what's happening to us—what we're doing."

"Yes. We should." My pleasure excited yet frightened me, and I worried about the possible consequences. We climbed down from that upper bunk, pulled on our robes and house shoes, quietly opened the door, and walked down the deserted hallway to the stairs that led to a small prayer room in the basement of the dormitory. There, we sat about four feet apart in straight-backed chairs facing each other.

Karen said, "What we just did is wrong."

Though I stated, "Yes, it was," I'd never actually felt it was wrong. It was so natural and felt so good. I'd always hidden its wrongness from myself. But now a part of me knew Karen was right.

I'd always been the perfect daughter, doing the right things, saying the right things, being the individual others looked up to. I'd never before done anything truly wrong, and my world crashed down on me that night.

Karen said, "The Bible teaches against this. A lot of verses prohibit what we feel toward each other, especially in Leviticus."

Both she and I were familiar with the instructions and admonitions of the Bible, the rules drilled into us from childhood. However, no one had ever discussed this particular subject openly with either of us. I didn't even know a word to use for it, yet a part of me halfheartedly acknowledged we had done a wicked thing.

The love I felt for Karen was forbidden. "But how can love be evil?" I asked myself. I loved her with all my being, all my soul. How can love be wrong? But yes, according to the Bible, it was. In God's eyes, we were sinning, breaking His law.

As we sat in those chairs facing each other in that little prayer room, we acknowledged that fact to each other. Karen bowed her head and said, "Then we need to stop what we're doing."

"Yes, we should," I said. Then I hesitated and gazed at her. "But I don't want to." I smiled.

"Neither do I." A happy, goofy grin spread across her face.

"I'm in love with you."

"And I'm in love with you."

We radiated happiness. Those were our marriage vows, as no others were allowed to us. She was my other half.

Falling in love with a girl stunned me. Even though I'd dated quite a few boys, I'd never fallen in love with one. *Why* was I drawn to a girl? Why had I fallen in love with one? When I'd wanted to kiss my high-school friend, Jean, at the drive-in movie, I never gave it a second thought because I'd never heard the words "gay," "lesbian," "homosexual," "queer," or "fag." The only word I'd ever heard was "sodomy," always spoken in such hushed tones I'd concluded it was something nasty that men did to each other. I couldn't even imagine what that "something nasty" was! I was totally ignorant of the possibility of two people of the same sex falling in love with each other.

Perhaps if I'd been aware this could happen, I would have avoided lying in bed with Karen as we conversed in whispers each night. If we'd never gotten in bed together, as innocent as it was in the beginning, would we have fallen in love anyway? I don't know. But I'm glad we did.

Chapter Two

Christmas vacation separated Karen and me for the first time. At Thanksgiving, I'd taken her home with me to Big Spring, as she didn't have enough time to visit her parents in Chicago. But Christmas was another story. I saw her off on the train, knowing I'd miss her terribly but confident I'd see her again.

This wouldn't be our final parting, though we knew it would eventually come. We never deluded ourselves about the future. We were in a bittersweet time—enjoying each other on a temporary basis. We couldn't spend our lives together. Occasionally we alluded to the possibility, but common sense always took over. Two girls, at least none we knew, just didn't do that.

We assumed it would be difficult for us to hold a decent job if we stayed together. We might even find it difficult to buy a home together. Society had set up too many barriers for us. We didn't know anyone to share our problem with, no books to read on the subject. We assumed no one else faced what we faced. We made our decision based solely on our religious upbringing, especially the admonition to honor our father and mother.

Neither of us wanted to hurt or embarrass our parents, who were highly respected individuals. They expected us to marry and have children. This was our lot in life. Our relationship had to remain a secret—from everyone.

My parents had always wanted me to be a teacher. I could be a teacher, a nurse, a secretary, or an airline stewardess. Those were my options. No one had ever mentioned any other possibility to me. Now I wish I'd taken my math skills seriously. Nursing appealed to me—helping others. Being an airline stewardess also appealed—traveling all over the world. But I chose secretarial work because I excelled in typing and shorthand. I could organize well—and secretaries need to be organized. I thought I'd enjoy running an office.

My parents, however, continued to encourage me to at least get my teaching certificate. "You may never have to use it," they explained to me, "but it's the best insurance policy you can ever have. If something ever happened to your husband, you could always support yourself and your family by teaching."

Even as they recommended my career choice, they were also letting me know they assumed I would marry and have children. Not until my third year of college did I begin to take their admonitions seriously and start taking education courses.

Regardless, though, of what careers Karen and I chose to follow, we would jeopardize those careers by living together.

We missed each other terribly that first Christmas vacation, so much so that we wrote long letters to each other every evening. Warning bells told me not to mail a letter to Karen every day, so I saved three or four days' worth of letters before putting them in an envelope to mail.

Even so, my parents became suspicious. Dad had majored in sociology and been introduced to the possibility of same-sex love. One night he told Mother,

"I think we have a problem with Lou Anne. Those long letters she writes to Karen every day indicate she may have fallen in love with her."

Mother was aghast. "Surely not, oh surely not!"

"Yes," he replied. "I think that's what has happened. You need to go in and talk with her about this."

And one night, as I sat propped up in bed writing a letter to Karen, that's just what Mother did. She sat down on my other twin bed just a couple of feet away from me and haltingly broached the subject of same-sex love. She mentioned a relative she believed had gone through life with his male companion. Her words made it clear that such a friendship was sinful and that Karen and I needed to separate. I don't recall her ever using the word "homosexual." That word possibly wasn't even in vogue.

The conversation was pretty much one-sided as she wanted me to "confess" to a relationship with Karen. I was embarrassed that she and Dad knew. Devastated. At one point Mother asked, "Which one of you is the male in your lovemaking?"

I was speechless. I had no idea what she was talking about. "What do you mean?" I finally asked.

"Normally, one of the girls plays the role of the male. Which role do you play? Are you a top or a bottom?"

My mouth probably flew open. Karen and I didn't play any roles. We just loved each other. The longer she talked, the more condemnation I felt. I was terribly embarrassed but also wanted her to understand my predicament, to sympathize with me. After all, Karen and I hadn't planned to fall in love! I was heartsick. I'd fallen deeply, everlastingly in love with someone I'd eventually have to part from. We'd never be able to marry, to have a family, to simply share life. How much worse could it get?

The feelings of guilt Mother evoked in me weren't new. I desperately needed my mother to put her arms around me, to tell me how sorry she was that I was suffering in this way, and to offer help. If she'd done that, I would have unburdened myself, shared everything, but that didn't happen. Consequently, I never admitted anything.

I loved Karen with all my being and knew of no way to suppress that love, to make it disappear. How much better if I'd fallen in love with a boy—someone my parents would approve of and someone I could marry and with whom I could have children. However, I'd fallen in love with a girl and been shown that evening the condemnation society would display if Karen and I didn't keep our relationship a secret. We'd always been careful, but now I grew afraid and became even more so as time passed.

The next day I called Karen to tell her the news. "Mother knows about us."

Karen was as shocked as I was. "Have you saved all the letters I've written you?"

"Yes. They're in a shoe box in my closet."

"You shouldn't have. Burn them immediately. I bet your mother has read them. Don't save any of my letters!"

I'd never suspected that my mother might read my letters, but I did as Karen ordered. I so hated to burn those letters, to never again be able to read her wonderful words of love, but I did. All of them. I never knew if Mother read them. I never asked, and she never mentioned them. Perhaps she didn't even know the letters were in my closet, but I destroyed them anyway, just in case.

After Mother confronted me, I became much more secretive. I didn't speak to her for days, angry that she'd confronted me, that she knew, that she'd condemned me, and that she wanted to separate Karen and me. But most of all I was angry at her lack of understanding sympathy. I hated her and became anxious for the holidays to end so I could return to the dorm and to Karen.

Somehow Karen and I continued our affair all spring, with a third roommate in the same room and three suite mates next door. I don't know if we were unusually discreet, if the others were just dumb, or if they had some idea of what was going on. No one ever said a word. The summer after our freshman year was a long, long summer apart from Karen. I missed her terribly but stayed busy working at Cosden Oil Refinery, where I substituted for various secretaries when they took their two-week summer vacations.

Just a week or two before classes were to begin at Baylor, I received a devastating letter from Karen. She would remain at home for the fall semester. She'd decided we should end our affair. This should give us time to make a clean break.

I wanted her to be happy; if she felt that our being together was wrong, then I was willing to go along with her plan to end our relationship. I didn't argue with her. Instead I told myself, "If she can make the break, then I can, too." We'd always felt guilty, convinced that our deep love was sinful. We'd always known our relationship could never be permanent. So I told myself that the three months of summer plus the four months of the fall semester would give me time to heal and overcome my desire to be with her.

I spent the fall semester telling myself I could live without Karen, convincing myself I never again needed to touch her. And, by January 1958, when Karen returned, I felt I'd succeeded. With both of us determined to end the affair, we could do it. After all, we were just separating a little sooner than we'd originally thought necessary.

When Karen arrived at Baylor, I was rooming with an art major. She and I had little in common, but we got along fine as roommates. Karen was assigned to a room with no roommate. Although the room contained bunk beds, it was considered a single room because it was so small. Karen had stopped by my room to greet me, but we'd been apart the rest of the day. Evening came, and I went to bed. My roommate went right to sleep. My bed was very close to the hall door, and as I dozed off, I suddenly realized Karen was kneeling by my bed. Touching my hand she asked, "Aren't you coming to my room?"

"I thought you decided we should stay apart," I whispered. "I've thought about it a lot and am willing to give it a try. If we both work at it, we can make the break."

Her reply amazed me. "You're the only reason I returned to school. If we can't be together, I'm leaving on the train tomorrow. I came back to be with you. I love you so very much. Don't do this to me."

By then she was grasping my hand, imploring me to come to her room. My resolve melted—because it was based on doing what I thought she wanted. But I'd either misread her, or she'd changed her mind without letting me know. Yet nothing would make me happier than going with her to her room.

All my mental anguish had been useless. Although

our long separation had provided a perfect opportunity to end our affair, that reasoning vanished now. I would have done anything for her. Certainly anything to make her happy. With only a moment's hesitation, I climbed out of bed and followed her.

Chapter Three

The next day I asked the dorm mother if I could change rooms and be Karen's roommate. "No," she replied. "That space is too small for two people."

"We don't mind," I assured her. "We really would like to be together."

"Is there a problem with the girl you're now with?" she asked.

"Not at all. She's very nice, and we get along just fine. It's just that Karen and I are good friends and enjoy being together. We really do want to room together."

The dorm mother then turned to Karen. "Is this something you want? Do you agree with this request?"

"Yes. I'd really like for Lou Anne to be with me."

"Well, the accommodation is too small for two, but if you want, I'll assign both of you to it."

We were elated. Karen and I spent some of our happiest times in that tiny dorm room, which we kept the rest of our sophomore year and all of our junior year.

❧❧❧❧

I continued to date boys on a regular basis, and during my junior year I dated a senior named Eric McGill, whose father was a Baptist preacher in West Texas. Eric had little money. He struggled to make ends meet and worked in one of the dining halls in order to pay his bills. He could afford to attend Baylor only because of the allowance available to P.K.s (preachers' kids). Consequently, when Eric and I dated, we always just walked around campus, had a Coke, and attended a free campus event or, occasionally, a movie. We seldom ate out.

One evening as we were strolling across campus, he said, "You're one of the few girls I've ever dated who doesn't expect me to spend a lot of money on a date. You and I have fun just doing simple things, and you don't realize how much I appreciate it."

"Spending a lot of money on me isn't necessary, Eric. I enjoy going out with you." And I did—up to a point. When I sensed a fellow was falling for me and wanted to hold and kiss me or, even worse, marry me, I was ready to turn him loose and look for someone else to date. But until Eric made the comment about inexpensive dating, I'd never thought about it, one way or the other. What we did together wasn't that important.

One evening we double-dated with his roommate, Jeff Tatum, and then Jeff asked me out. I accepted, and we dated a few times. Then Eric called. "Lou Anne, I like you a lot, and I'd like to continue dating you, but if you prefer going with Jeff, I understand and will step aside."

I hadn't thought about Eric in a serious way, but he'd obviously thought seriously about me. It was probably good that he was willing to back off and allow me to date Jeff. "Thanks, Eric," I said. "I do like you, but I need to think about this. You really are a great guy."

He said again that he wouldn't stand in Jeff's way and wished me the best. I appreciated his attitude, and Jeff and I ended up dating rather exclusively. But Eric remained in the picture as the three of us worked together to help establish a little Baptist church just outside Waco. I played the piano when no one else was available, and Jeff and Eric took turns preaching and leading the singing. We met in a family's small three-bedroom home. Bedrooms became Sunday-school classrooms, and the den and kitchen area was the sanctuary.

One of the tragedies of being gay and having to keep it a secret is hurting others. Jeff fell deeply in love with me, and I liked him a lot. But I couldn't fall in love with him, much less spend my life with him. I was in love with Karen.

Jeff asked me to marry him, and this wasn't the only proposal I turned down—certainly not the only heart I broke. How much better if I could have been open about my sexual orientation.

༄ ༄ ༄ ༄

While I was dating Jeff, Karen had become interested in a senior in her psychology class, Russell Hampton. I became accustomed to hearing, "I'm heading to the library to study. Russell may be there. Don't wait up for me."

Returning from the library, she was either down, because Russell hadn't shown up, or elated because he had. Occasionally, she'd be in the clouds because he'd asked her to the student union to have a Coke.

I wasn't jealous of Russell. After all, I dated boys and had dated them all the time Karen and I were together. But Karen had never dated. She saw herself as overweight and therefore undesirable. The truth was, she had no experience being with boys and no self-confidence along that line. Her mother had convinced her that no boy would pay any attention to her until she lost some weight. The more critical her mother became, the more Karen ate. The two of them battled constantly when they were together.

Karen's skin was unblemished, her makeup flawless, and her hair carefully coiffed. A large-boned blonde of German descent, she probably weighed 135 to 140 pounds. I really didn't know, and I didn't care. I just knew that I loved her and yearned for her to feel good about herself.

Although I felt no jealousy toward Russell, I began to dislike him because he never asked Karen out on a date. He would hint to her after their psychology class that he might study in the library that evening and maybe they could study together. That's all it took for her to spend the evening sitting there, hoping he'd show. And sometimes he would come, though sometimes he wouldn't. Helplessly, I watched her infatuation with him begin to control her emotions. The more he took over her thoughts, the less she wanted to be with me. She finally informed me, "I'm in love with Russell. Your relationship with me must end. I don't want us touching each other any more. I realize this won't be easy for you, especially with us rooming together, but it's time. I don't want us to even hold hands any more."

I was devastated. She was my very life, and she was rejecting me. Just a year before, I'd been willing to halt our relationship, but she'd convinced me not to. Now the shoe was on the other foot, and I couldn't handle it.

I was so accustomed to cuddling with her at night, to sleeping next to her in that single bunk bed, that I couldn't go to sleep by myself. I thought constantly about her, about being with her, touching her, sleeping with her. When we turned out the lights each night, I'd be in the bottom bunk, she just above me in the top one. I wanted so much to hold her, yet after she told me not to touch her again, I didn't. I never forced any attention on her, but not because I didn't want to. I loved her terribly, completely, and was miserable.

This was the first time someone had totally rejected me. One night, beside myself, I begged, and Karen ignored me. I told her I was going to kill myself, but she didn't take me seriously, so I headed for the bathroom and found her bottle of sleeping pills. I emptied the bottle and swallowed all thirteen pills. "That's not going to kill you," she said. "Those pills aren't strong enough."

She was right. With a lot of effort on her part, I awakened the next morning. "Wake up," she kept saying as she shook me. "You have to get up. You have a date to the football game, and you need to get up and dress."

I felt absolutely awful, like I was in a stupor. I could hardly hold my head up, but it never occurred to me to cancel my date. I dressed, but not with any wisdom as I wore a sweater when the weather turned out to be warm. My date brought me a corsage, and I had great difficulty pinning it to my sweater. The heavy corsage drooped down from my loosely knit teal-blue sweater. It didn't look right, but I couldn't very well change clothes with my date standing there ready to go.

The game was a blur. I had a terrible time just staying awake. I was miserable. Ill. Hot. Uncomfortable. I recall nothing of the game, even less of my date. He never asked me out again.

While Karen wanted nothing to do with me, I quietly cried myself to sleep most nights—those nights I was able to get to sleep. I couldn't sleep alone but finally devised a plan that provided me a few hours' sleep. After we turned out the lights, I waited until Karen was asleep, then quietly crawled up into her bunk and curled up at the foot of her bed. Just barely touching one of her feet, I was able to sleep. I awakened before she did in the mornings and returned to my bed without her knowing I'd slept with her. At least I assumed she never knew.

Our little dorm room was probably ten by ten. Besides the bunk beds, it held only a chest of drawers and a small desk and chair. We had our own tiny bath, which was much better than having a larger one shared by up to six girls.

We'd spent many happy hours in that little room, but now, as we shared this cramped space in the first semester of our junior year, we avoided touching each other. We both felt the strain. My love for Karen continued. I hated Russell. If he'd shown a normal interest in her, I probably wouldn't have disliked him. More than anything, I wanted her to be happy. We were convinced we would find happiness in marriage and family, so I wanted her to find someone good and loving to marry. But Russell never asked her out on a date, never took her out to eat, to a movie, or to any campus gathering. In no way did he show her off as someone special to him. He just furtively met her at the library and occasionally bought her a Coke. I knew this wasn't a normal courtship, but Karen didn't. She was smitten.

I couldn't tell her Russell wasn't treating her right. I realized what he was doing to her and hated him for leading her on. The little bit of attention Russell gave her was enough to cause her to fall in love. He was her first beau. Occasionally I'd try to warn her about him, but I couldn't do so very often or she'd think I was just being a sore loser. I stayed very concerned.

Chapter Four

At Christmas of my junior year I was dating both Eric and Jeff. Both of them gave me a ride home to Big Spring in West Texas for that long holiday period, as Jeff planned to spend the time off with Eric, whose family had recently moved to Big Spring. I recall sitting in the front seat of the car between the two of them, the three of us laughing and talking and simply having fun.

Eric said, "I bet Russell's excited about now."

"Yeah. It's been months since he's seen Donna. They have a lot of planning to do over the holidays," Jeff added.

"Isn't their wedding supposed to take place two weeks after he graduates?" Eric asked.

"Yeah. He sure is crazy about her," Jeff said. "Talks about her all the time."

I was appalled. "Are you talking about Russell Hampton?"

"Yes."

"He's engaged to be married?"

"Yes. For years. Won't be much longer now."

"But I have a friend who likes him. She has no idea he's engaged!"

"Oh, I know," Eric replied. "He's just experimenting with her as part of those psychology courses he's taking. We've been telling him he shouldn't do her that way, but he won't listen."

For the first time I realized these three fellows roomed together. Years later it dawned on me that Eric and Jeff had probably planned that conversation because they felt sorry for Karen and the way Russell was treating her. But back then I couldn't grasp anything except the fact that Russell was duping, using, and treating Karen unmercifully.

At first, I didn't believe them, but then I reminded myself that Russell had never asked Karen out on a real date. How could anyone treat another human being in such a callous, cruel manner? Karen was convinced Russell cared for her and was picturing wedding bells with him. What he was doing to her was unforgivable. The cad!

I don't recall the rest of that drive. I couldn't think about anything but Karen and the heartbreak ahead for her. Should I tell her? Obviously, I had to. If the shoe were on the other foot, I'd want to know the truth. I couldn't allow this to continue. But how could I warn her? Would she hate me? That didn't matter. She had to know. I began mentally writing her a letter, revising it in my mind.

After several days passed, I finally wrote something like this.

Karen, being good friends usually means sharing happy times together. Occasionally, however, being a good friend requires one to be honest about a painful truth. Please know that what I'm about to tell you brings me no joy or happiness, only sorrow and anguish. I say these things with tears in my eyes, knowing how much my words are about to hurt you.

I then related to her what Jeff and Eric had told

me about Russell as kindly, as gently, as considerately as possible. "I'm aware how terribly hurt you must now feel," I wrote in conclusion.

I understand if you're angry with me and hope you don't dislike me, but I have to be truthful regardless of the consequences. I care for you very much and am sorry to give you such painful news.

During the remainder of the holiday, I heard nothing from Karen. Today, I would have picked up the phone to check on her, but in the '50s, our family rarely made long-distance calls because of the expense. Calling her wasn't an option. Besides, I didn't know if she'd even talk with me. I had no idea how she was taking the news about Russell or whether she even believed me. Would she think I was just trying to win her back? No, she wouldn't think that because we trusted each other.

When the holidays were over, I hitched a ride back to school with Jeff and Eric. They lived in an off-campus apartment and needed to return a day or two early because of their work schedule. But I never thought to ask if the dormitories would be open. I just assumed they would be, but they weren't. We were all surprised. There I was, in Waco, with no place to spend the night. My only alternative was to go to the downtown hotel.

Eric and Jeff carried my luggage into the hotel lobby, and I checked in. Jeff asked me to go out to eat, then to a movie, and I accepted. With only a little over an hour before he'd be back to pick me up, I headed to my room to freshen up from our 300-mile drive. Since boys didn't go up to a girl's hotel room, I arranged to meet him in the lobby at six thirty.

As we were about to leave the hotel, Karen walked

in. "What are you doing here?" I asked.

"My train arrived today, and the dorms aren't open. I'm staying here tonight."

"Me, too. Eric and Jeff gave me a ride back. I never dreamed the dorms would be closed. So here I am!"

"Where are you going?" she asked, looking at Jeff and me.

"Out to eat and to a movie."

"Come see me when you get back. I'm in Room 342."

"Okay."

I wanted to visit her right then, to immediately go up to her room to see how she was doing, to find out how she took the news about Russell. I was mad at myself for having made the date with Jeff and resented the evening with him. The dinner seemed to take too long, and the movie took even longer. Even then, he wasn't ready to take me back. Finally, about ten thirty, I told him I was tired, and he reluctantly returned me to the hotel. Of course, I headed immediately to Karen's room and knocked on her door. She opened it right away and said, "You certainly weren't in any hurry to get here!"

"I'm sorry. I'd already made the date and couldn't back out at the last minute."

"I know. I've just been anxious to see you." She was wearing her pajamas and robe and climbed back in bed, propping herself up with pillows against the headboard. I followed the no-touching rules she'd set and sat down on the floor, leaning back against the bed.

Soon, she gently placed a hand on my shoulder. "Thank you for the kindest letter I've ever received. I read and reread it and realized that, despite the horrible news, you told me in the most loving way possible. I even showed your letter to Mother. She agreed that it was the kindest letter she'd ever read and told me how lucky I am to have you for a friend. She's right. Thank you."

Delighted to feel her touch as well as to hear her loving words, I explained. "I hope you realize I never wanted to write that letter. I never liked Russell and the way he led you on, but I felt so sad when I learned what he was doing to you. I'd do almost anything to keep you from being hurt like this." Tears were in my eyes and in my voice.

"I'm all right," she said. "Yes, it hurt. Very badly. But I'm over it. I really am." Then she touched me on the cheek. "Would you stay with me tonight? I want you to spend the night with me. I'm so sorry for the way I've treated you."

What glorious words. Joy flooded my total being. She wanted me back! And the setting was ideal—a hotel room that gave us complete privacy. Rising from the floor, I turned, leaned over, and kissed her, then lay down beside her. Touching her, holding her, kissing her brought heaven down into my heart. After a short while, she suggested, "Go get your things from your room and move in with me."

"Are you sure?"

"Yes, I want you with me. I've treated you terribly. Please forgive me. I love you so much. Hurry. Don't take long. I want you back here soon."

"I'll hurry," I promised

Going to my room, I gathered up my luggage, mussed up my bed to make it look as if I'd slept in it, then quickly returned to Karen's room. What a marvelous night. We stayed in each other's arms throughout the night and long into the morning.

Chapter Five

That last semester together was bittersweet. Karen's dad planned to spend the next year overseas and asked Karen to go with him. The opportunity was too good to pass up, so plans were made for her to complete her degree out of the country. We talked little about our future together. We had no future. We'd always known that. Consequently, the subject rarely came up. We learned to treasure the time we had together and accepted the fact we would part in the very near future.

Whenever I face something unpleasant, I avoid talking about it. I suppose I think that if I don't talk about it, don't acknowledge its presence, it'll disappear. That's the way I treated my eventual separation from Karen. We each kept our feelings about the future close to our hearts and seldom mentioned the inevitable farewell. For two individuals who delighted in discussing each and every subject, we certainly avoided this subject.

❧ ❧ ❧ ❧

The last semester of my junior year, Jeff was becoming quite serious about me and sent me a bouquet of red and white carnations for Valentine's Day. This was quite a splurge for him. He proposed to me, and I turned him down. Nevertheless, he continued to date me. Several weeks before he graduated, we were parked in some remote area and he asked me to lie down beside him on the front seat of the car.

"No," I replied. "I don't want to do that."

"I promise not to do anything funny. You can trust me. I just want to feel you lying beside me."

I already felt guilty for not accepting his proposal, so against my better judgment, I did as he requested. I felt so uncomfortable there beside him that my body was rigid as I waited to see what would happen. True to his word, though, he just held me and kissed me. I continued to feel uncomfortable and could hardly wait to sit back up.

When we did, he said, "I know you've already told me you won't marry me, but I want to show you what I've already bought for you." He then reached in his pocket and handed me a little box.

The diamond engagement ring made me want to cry for him. I knew exactly what it was like to love someone and not have that love returned. I could imagine how miserable he was, but I would be miserable married to him. I wished I were in love with him, as he would have been a wonderful person to marry. But I wasn't and probably did him a big favor by turning down his proposal.

Several years after that evening, when I was a high-school teacher in Odessa, Texas, Jeff called me. He was now living in California but presently visiting in West Texas, and he asked, "May I stop by and see you tomorrow?"

"Of course. I'd love to see you."

He came to my apartment, kissed me, and we sat down and visited. After asking how I was doing, he said, "I'm engaged to a girl I met in California. However, I wanted to come by and see you first, to see if you might change your mind about marrying me. If so, I won't marry this girl."

"No, Jeff, there's no chance. I'm sorry."

"I am, too. But I need to buy a pair of shoes for my wedding. Will you go shopping with me?"

"Sure!"

So off we went to downtown Odessa, going in one store after another to look for just the right shoes. As we walked down the sidewalk, he held my hand every chance he got. "How strange," I thought. "He's buying shoes for his wedding but holding *my* hand." But I figured it wouldn't hurt anything to let him do that, so I didn't stop him. He eventually found the shoes he was looking for, bought them, took me back to my apartment, and left.

I didn't see him again for many, many years. His marriage lasted for quite some time, but they eventually divorced and he remarried.

⟡⟡⟡⟡

But back to my junior year in college. Soon after the school year ended, I took a train to Chicago to spend the summer with Karen. Because she would be out of the country all the next year, my parents relented and let me spend the summer with her. But first they established some ground rules. From all the indications, they informed Karen's parents of our relationship and asked them to keep an eye on us and prohibit our being together privately.

Although I'd met Karen's dad when he made a trip to Texas, I'd never met her mother, who, when seeing me for the first time, exclaimed, "Oh, how beautiful you are! What a tiny waist! I've never seen such a tiny waist.

It must not be more than eighteen inches!"

"Oh, it's more than that," I replied. "Probably closer to twenty-four."

"Oh, no. It couldn't be! It looks much smaller than that."

I was embarrassed, not just for myself but for Karen. I knew how important a small figure was to Karen's mother, who was a small-boned woman, unlike Karen. The more compliments she piled on me, the more obvious it became that she was trying to draw Karen's attention to her need to lose some weight. I was 5'4" and weighed about 110 pounds, whereas Karen was 5'5" and weighed about 140 pounds. But we were built differently. Trying to compare the two of us was unfair. "You're just like Scarlett O'Hara!" Mrs. Mundt exclaimed. "A real Southern belle!" Her mother's delight in my appearance was her way of saying to Karen, "Look at her! Why can't you be like that?"

That comparison made for a very uncomfortable atmosphere. Karen told me that evening, after she and her mother had a few moments to talk, that her mother had said, "No wonder Lou Anne chose you for a friend. She knows you'll never give her any competition with the boys."

"Karen," I said, "you know better than that. Don't give her words a second thought. They're just not true and you know it."

"Yes, but it still hurts."

"Of course it does. That was cruel. I can't believe a mother would say that to her daughter."

Karen's bedroom, which contained twin beds, was just off the living room. When time came for everyone to go to bed, Karen's mother began bringing covers and pillows into the living room and putting them on the sofa. "You two girls leave your bedroom door open tonight," she said. "I'm going to sleep on the sofa so I can keep an eye on you."

That's when I knew Mother was bound to have called and told Karen's mother about our relationship and asked her to keep us separated. It was uncomfortable and embarrassing to know she was watching us. We left the door open and stayed in our own beds, making no effort to touch each other. However, Mrs. Mundt got up several times during the night to check on us. She just peered in at us, then went back to her bed on the sofa. Nothing else was ever said about our relationship.

Karen and I were determined to do nothing to arouse suspicion. We were perfect and never broke the unspoken rules. After less than a week, Mrs. Mundt returned to her and her husband's bedroom, and Karen and I continued to leave the bedroom door open and to stay apart. Even during the day, we sat cross-legged on our individual beds to talk. We were determined to do nothing that might result in my being sent home. The only times we touched each other were when both parents were out of the apartment, and even then we stayed alert.

I suppose our exemplary behavior convinced Karen's parents that what they'd been told about us was untrue, because they eventually left for a month's stay in their small cabin in the woods of northern Michigan. Karen was taking a summer-school class at Northwestern University, so we couldn't accompany them; and I was doing temporary work in various offices to help pay my expenses. Her parents, I'm sure, needed some time alone prior to the upcoming year-long trip Dr. Mundt and Karen would soon be making overseas. Karen's mother would remain in Chicago as a public-school counselor, and they were probably dreading the long separation.

When Karen's parents left for Michigan, we were ecstatic because we had the apartment all to ourselves. Fifteen minutes after the Mundts walked out the door, Karen and I grinned at each other and headed toward her parents' bed.

Those weeks we were alone in the apartment were like a honeymoon. We bought each other flowers and strawberry cheesecake (which I'd never eaten before). Our days together were idyllic, wonderful. We took long walks along Michigan Avenue and sometimes even held hands, not caring who saw us. On days when I wasn't working, I accompanied Karen to Northwestern University and sat on the shore of Lake Michigan reading while she attended class. We went shopping, rode the subway and the EL, went to movies, visited the zoo, ate out at restaurants, went to museums, and enjoyed every minute we had together.

One day Karen met some of her former high-school friends for lunch, eager to introduce me to them. My Southern accent intrigued them, as they kept asking, "Say something. Anything. Just talk." And I'd comply. Naturally, I found their accents a little odd, but they sounded just like Karen, and by then, I'd become accustomed to her speech. I happily entertained her friends, saying whatever came to mind.

When Karen completed her class, her parents called and instructed us to take a bus and join them in their cabin, situated on a small lake. The little rustic cabin was nice, containing a living room, a downstairs bedroom with a loft bedroom just above it, and a tiny kitchen. No electricity. No running water, but there was a water pump next to the kitchen sink. The Mundts used the downstairs bedroom. Karen and I had the loft, which opened onto the living room.

During our time together in the Michigan woods we took long walks every day. Never before had I seen a birch tree and was amazed at the color of the bark and how it peeled off. The unusual, beautiful trees were so unlike the trees I was familiar with in Texas. The woods gave us solitude and privacy, and we often held hands as we walked through them. We used a small rowboat to explore the tiny lake. Then in the evenings, as a hush fell, Karen, her parents, and I would gather in the living room to read, visit, or play games. Often I'd sit cross-legged on the floor and play my flute.

Neither Karen nor I seemed to comprehend that these days together in the Michigan woods were our last ones together. We never discussed that fact. When we returned to the city, we left the bedroom door open at all times and never touched each other when a parent was in the apartment. Everyone began preparing for Karen's upcoming trip with her father. Karen and I shopped a lot during that period of time, and she had to go have the required vaccinations. I went everywhere with her and helped her pack. Still, as we worked together, neither of us voiced the question that remained buried below our conscious thoughts: "Will we ever see each other again?"

Why did we never address this question? Even now, tears come as I think about seeing her off on the plane and not realizing how empty my life would be. I wished her a safe trip, a happy year—the type of good-bye I'd say to anyone. I recall only a numbness, an emptiness, as Mrs. Mundt and I stood in O'Hare Airport until the plane was off the ground. Then, without a word, we turned and left the airport. She, I'm certain, had her own sad thoughts. After all, she would be totally alone for a year. Even though she'd have her job to keep her occupied, she'd be coming home to an empty apartment every night.

My thoughts? I don't know. I seemed to have no feelings, no thoughts. I couldn't afford to let my emotions show to Karen's mother, so I remained stoic. This experience initiated my training in detaching myself from my emotions, which I became quite adept at.

Mrs. Mundt took me out to eat that night, then to a movie. We saw a new release, *Gunfight at the O.K. Corral*, starring Kirk Douglas, and I've never wanted to see that movie again. The following day Mrs. Mundt drove me to the train station, and I headed home.

Chapter Six

After I graduated from Baylor in 1960, I was awarded a teaching assistantship at The University of Texas in Austin. This position allowed me to teach typewriting and shorthand as I worked on my master's degree in management. Because I'd waited until I was a junior at Baylor to begin work on my teaching certificate, I took those additional education courses at the same time I worked on my master's and was able to graduate by the end of the next summer with a teaching certificate as well as an MBA.

As I began seeking a job as a teacher, I thought it would be nice to live within visiting distance of my parents, but definitely not in the same town. They were still in Big Spring, almost 300 miles west of Dallas. I accepted a position teaching in Odessa, sixty miles west of Big Spring—close but not too close. Several weeks after I signed a contract, my parents informed me they were moving to Little Rock, 670 miles from Odessa. I was shocked. I knew absolutely no one in Odessa, but Mother helped me locate an apartment, and that fall I began teaching business classes at Odessa High School.

I was twenty-two, most of my classmates from high school were married, and my mother was concerned that I didn't have a steady beau. Quite often when I'd come home on weekends from Baylor or the University of Texas, she would have arranged a blind date for me.

She was certainly doing her part to help me find a

husband. And I'd always known that marriage was part of my future. It was simply a given.

My parents had two goals for me: to earn my teaching certificate and then to get married. I never questioned this societal standard. By the time I was twenty-three, I told myself to just pick out a nice fellow, marry him, and get it over with. Not long after I made this decision, a friend arranged a blind date for me.

Jim was a nice fellow, a schoolteacher with aspirations to be a school administrator. This goal appealed to me, as my dad was a school administrator. Jim's dad was a Southern Baptist minister. He loved children and wanted to have a family. I very much wanted to have children, so I asked myself, "What more am I looking for? He fits the bill." We were married in March 1963.

Less than three years after we married, I realized I'd made a terrible mistake. I wanted out of the marriage but never said a word to anyone about it. I was miserably unhappy, but my parents and my church had taught me that marriage is forever, an unbreakable commitment. By the time I began to seriously consider divorce, we'd had our first son and named him after his dad. I told myself it would be cruel to separate Jim from his young namesake he was so proud of. They were crazy about each other.

Then I thought of my parents. Dad and Mom would be so hurt and embarrassed to have their only daughter a divorcée. I couldn't do that to them because divorcing in the '60's was shameful. Jim's parents, who had accepted me as if I were their own daughter, were so proud of me, and so loving. Divorcing their eldest son would be a terrible blow. Siblings on both sides of the family would be hurt.

Each time I contemplated asking for a divorce, thoughts such as these came to mind. The only one who would benefit from a divorce would be me. I'd been taught all my life not to be selfish, and I couldn't break that ingrained pattern. So I ultimately decided to honor my wedding vows, "till death do us part."

We eventually had four children, and they brought light and joy into my life, and still do. When the first child was a boy, I was delighted, as was Jim. We both wanted a son. My second pregnancy ended in a spontaneous abortion after four and a half months. Then I became pregnant with our second child. At this time, I begged God to give me another boy, though Jim kept reminding me of how much he wanted a daughter. But I didn't want one because I didn't trust myself with a daughter. My fears were ridiculous but had something to do with my strange feelings toward girls. I didn't understand *why* I had them and didn't know there was a name for people like me. I kept my head buried in the sand by never reading about homosexuality, never discussing it with anyone except that horrible time my mother condemned me for my feelings about Karen.

I didn't want to take a chance on having strange feelings toward a daughter and constantly begged God for a son. My prayer was answered. Our second child was a boy. A little over a year later, I again became pregnant. Jim definitely wanted a daughter this time, but I never told him how desperately I was praying for another boy.

Thank goodness, we had a third son. Jim was terribly disappointed, and guilt poured over me for having begged God for a boy. I was convinced then, and am convinced now, that our three boys resulted from my prayers. Despite Jim's disappointment, I was secretly delighted to have a third son.

I've always regarded my inability to love a man as God's dirty trick on me. At the same time, I'd tell myself, "God has tried to make up for the dirty trick He played on me by giving me a good life!" Not only did He grant my request for sons, but I'd married a fine man. By all outward appearances, I had an ideal, secure life.

As the three boys began to grow up, I realized the time would come when Jim and I would be alone in our home, just the two of us. I wasn't ready for that. The boys had always served as a buffer, as a means for me to avoid being alone with Jim. I wanted another child to prolong that buffer a while longer. However, I was reaching an age when few women continued to have children. The time had come to make a decision.

I approached Jim and asked, "Would you like to have another child?"

"Yes," he replied. "I'd love to have a daughter!"

Realizing we would probably have another boy, I warned him, "We can't go into this wanting a girl. The doctor told me our chances of having one are one in eight. We either go into this wanting another *child*, regardless of what sex it is, or we don't do it at all."

Jim immediately replied. "I want another child, regardless."

So we began trying to start a baby. I didn't get pregnant immediately. It took about a year, so that when our fourth child was born I was almost forty. I began considering the possibility of having a daughter. So many years had passed since I'd felt anything special toward a female that I considered myself finally all right. I began picturing how nice it would be to have a daughter with me in the kitchen, with whom to share thoughts and ideas, a companion. The more I thought about having a daughter, the more I wanted one, and I began praying. I even promised I'd never hurt this girl.

I know now that my fears regarding a daughter were ridiculous. But at the time, those fears were very real. I simply didn't understand myself.

Chapter Seven

Through the years, Jim and I struggled in our marriage. In 1985 we seriously discussed divorcing. One evening Jim called our sons Michael and Josh into our bedroom and informed them we were getting a divorce by simply explaining, "Your mother doesn't love me anymore." The boys were probably sixteen and fourteen at the time.

His statement and laying all the blame on me infuriated me, but I didn't say a word. I didn't believe in arguing in front of our children. These two boys were the only children at home at this time. Our eldest son, J.W., was attending Baylor, and seven-year-old Laura was in Little Rock for a two-week summer visit with my parents.

Soon afterward, only a few days into her visit, Laura became homesick and begged to come home. Because the drive from Austin to Little Rock is a long one—over 500 miles—we agreed to split the difference with my parents and meet them outside a cafeteria in Mount Pleasant, Texas. The day of that drive, Michael had other plans, so only Josh rode with us.

Prior to our arrival in Mt. Pleasant, we told Josh, "Give us a few minutes to visit with your grandmother and granddad and Laura. Then we'd like for you to take Laura a little ways off and play with her so your daddy and I can talk privately with your grandparents. We don't want Laura to hear of the divorce right now. We'll sit down and talk with her about it later."

"Sure, Mom," Josh replied. He, I knew, would do as we asked. All of us were quieter than usual that day. We didn't play our usual car games that helped make the time pass quickly and keep the atmosphere light and happy. None of us seemed to have much to say.

We made excellent connections in Mt. Pleasant. Laura, of course, was delighted to see us and kept clinging to me. But she was also pleased to see Josh, who was just as happy to see her. All the boys were crazy about her, and she felt the same about her three big brothers. I eventually suggested to Josh that he and Laura could walk over to another area and play for a few minutes. He took her hand and led her away, and we watched as they played chase.

Turning to Mother and Dad, I said, "Jim and I are planning to get a divorce."

"What?" They stared at us.

"Yes. We've already talked with Michael and Josh."

"But I don't understand!" Mother said. "Why?"

"We think it's best" was all I could come up with.

My parents just stood there, silent. Finally, Dad looked at me. "Lou Anne, does this decision make you happy?"

"No," I admitted. Although I wanted a divorce, I hated to break up the family. I dreaded telling everyone our marriage was over. I wasn't certain how I'd be able to support myself and the children. All I felt was misery, and guilt, lots of it. I was breaking my marriage vow, although I'd spent nearly every year of the marriage yearning for God to just take me so I could escape it.

Dad apparently took my admission to mean that I wasn't in favor of the divorce—which was the furthest possible thing from the truth. He looked at both of us. "You need to work this out. Find some way. Get counseling, but try to make a go of it. You two don't need to be doing this." Dad was superintendent of a huge school system, used to making decisions and giving directions.

I didn't know what to say. Forty-six at the time, I'd spent my life obeying either my father or my husband. Dad told me not to divorce and to try to make a go of it, so that's what I'd do. "All right," I said.

Jim and I didn't talk much as we drove home to Austin with two of our children in the car. We didn't want to discuss this subject in front of them.

We ended up not divorcing—primarily because each of us insisted the other contact a lawyer and start the proceedings. Neither of us did that, so the decision just died for lack of any action. But we were both very unhappy.

❧ ❧ ❧ ❧

After fifteen years in Austin, Jim accepted a job as a high-school principal in Tyler, located in East Texas. Living in a much smaller place appealed to both of us, so we moved there in 1988. Baptist churches seemed to abound on every corner, and the two largest ones began vying for our membership. We joined the smaller of the two, First Baptist Church. I immediately became active in various programs and especially enjoyed playing in their handbell choir. In 1999, I accepted a job teaching a ladies' Sunday-school class.

❧ ❧ ❧ ❧

One morning in August 1999, I slowly and quietly slid out of bed so I wouldn't awaken Jim. Little did I realize, as I slipped on my robe, that by the end of the day, my life would have totally changed.

The day began like any other Sunday morning as I used the quiet time to review the Sunday-school lesson I planned to teach to the women's class in this extremely conservative area of the state we call deep East Texas.

The church, over 150 years old, is an imposing structure located downtown. Prior to accepting this assignment, I'd occasionally worked with children, either in Sunday school or during Vacation Bible School. I found teaching adults more challenging as I felt anxious about each week's lesson, despite the ladies' reassurances that I was doing a great job. Consequently, I spent many hours preparing the lessons, certainly a lot more time than was needed, or expected.

The class was small. Quite small. Once seven attended, but three or four was the norm. Sometimes only one or two showed up, and once I was the only one there. These loving, kind, supportive ladies in their fifties, having struggled the previous year without a teacher, refused to disband or to be absorbed into another class. When I agreed to be their teacher, they joyfully welcomed me.

Upon arriving at church on this hot day, I climbed the stairs of the Education Building up to the fourth floor. At sixty, I reminded myself to take every opportunity to climb those stairs, because someday I'd no longer be able to do so. I was always challenging my 5'4" petite stature to remain energetic, both physically and mentally.

This particular Sunday I was selfishly disappointed when only one class member arrived, yet what happened to me that day would never have occurred if anyone else had appeared. At first I felt frustrated because I'd spent many hours preparing the lesson. Then I said, "Janie, it's difficult to teach a lesson to only one person, but I will. Otherwise, we can visit and get to know each other better."

"That's a great idea, Lou Anne," she replied. Janie, always smiling and animated, had a vast amount of energy bundled into a tiny body. Although she attended regularly, I knew little about her and asked how many children she had. Among women in their fifties, this topic is usually an excellent way to get to know someone.

During the next forty minutes we shared stories about our families, our lives, and our faith. We touched upon a variety of subjects, and my original opinion of Janie, that she was a very caring and tenderhearted person, was confirmed that morning.

As Janie began talking about her artist son, how caring and thoughtful he was, I felt certain he was gay—a homosexual. I can't explain the feeling but had no doubt in my mind. I believe God put that thought in my head and nudged me to do what I did next. I blurted out, "Is your son a homosexual?"

People simply don't ask that question in a conservative area like East Texas, and especially of a member of a Southern Baptist church. She hesitated quite a while, then stated in strong tones, "Yes, he is, but God loves him just the way he is. We, too, should love and accept homosexuals."

I was dumbfounded. Here I was, sixty years old, and I'd never heard a Christian say anything positive, loving, or accepting about homosexuals. Janie's words broke through the wall within me—the wall I'd carefully constructed to protect myself from the world. At that moment, her words had little impact on me because I felt no forewarning, no hint whatsoever of the devastation, of the uprooting of my carefully planned life her words would cause.

When our class time ended and we stood up to leave, Janie reached over to give me a hug in parting. I'd always avoided touching anyone, but Janie was a hugger, so I put my arms around her and briefly held her close, letting her long, blond hair brush against my face. Our bond began that morning.

ৡ৷ৡ৷ৡ৷ৡ

After cooking lunch for Jim and myself, cleaning up the dishes, and changing into more comfortable clothes, I returned to the kitchen to bake cinnamon bread. As I stood there mixing up the bread, my thoughts returned to my conversation with Janie.

Life had dealt her some damaging blows, so as I thought about some of her personal problems, sorrow swept through me. It amazed me to feel such pain for another person's problems. I'd always prided myself on being in control and seldom felt deep emotion, especially regarding problems not even my own. I'd never before experienced anything like what I was then feeling. Something peculiar was happening to me.

When I was only twenty, I'd deliberately disconnected my emotions, buried them very deep within me, and spent my life pretending to be someone I really wasn't. Over the years, I'd kept them so subdued that I'd eventually convinced myself they no longer existed. Now, forty years later, I thought I was in complete control. But this was a terrible mistake. I should have continued to be watchful. I should have never assumed that just because my emotions had been dormant all these years, they no longer existed.

I began to empathize with Janie, feeling profound sorrow for her. And then I began to cry. Tears streamed down my face.

Soon another thought came to me—just bounced into my mind. "Perhaps Janie and I can be friends." I'd lived my adult life avoiding close friendships to protect myself. Consequently, I'd never unburdened myself to anyone else, not even my husband.

But suddenly, something in Janie made me hope, made me yearn for a friendship I'd been missing. I saw in Janie a gentle spirit, an openness, and a loving attitude. I'd thoroughly enjoyed talking with her. She'd trusted me that morning as she shared personal problems, so I thought, "If she trusts me enough to share those difficulties, then perhaps I've found someone with whom to share my problems—someone who might actually understand me."

At last maybe I could open up and be honest about myself, admit to someone that I was gay. I hadn't realized until that afternoon what a burden I'd been carrying all my life, the burden of secrecy.

"What would it be like," I wondered, "to reveal myself to someone who would understand me, and hopefully accept me, knowing that I'm gay? Would I really have the nerve to be open and honest with her?"

As my mind jumped from one possibility to another, especially the possibility of having a real friend, my emotions suddenly changed directions—again. Instead of feeling happy about a possible friendship with Janie, I experienced a terrible pain, as if my heart were cracking open.

Anguish flooded through me, as if I were being

swept up in crashing torrents of agony. I'd lived for too many years keeping my past safely bottled up inside me. I was reconciled to always being alone. I'd become so secure that only occasionally did I bemoan the fact that my aloneness would go with me to the grave—no one would ever really know who I was.

Chapter Eight

I'd been at war with my body nearly all my life. Major battles some years, small skirmishes others, but always at war.

When I was a teenager, I refused to face the truth about myself, killing my soul, the being I was created to be. My emptiness grew as I blindly, and very successfully, played the role that society, church, and my family insisted was mine.

But they were wrong. They didn't know me. How could they when I didn't even know myself?

The mold that governed my life didn't fit. It hurt. It made me miserable. Simple existence, not happiness, had become my goal. I was convinced I could never be happy and often yearned for an early death as a means of escape.

Friends and family, looking upon me in this stage of my life, called me successful. My marriage had lasted for thirty-six years, my husband and I were respected members of the community, and our four children were healthy, kind, intelligent, good-looking, and college educated. My outward life gave no indication of my inward misery.

Dormant for so many years, my feelings suddenly sprang to life that Sunday afternoon. I was feeling emotion. Unwelcomed emotion. Unexpected emotion.

Caught by surprise, I was unprepared to handle it. I didn't understand what was happening inside me.

Sorrow cascaded over me, overwhelmed me. Tears streamed down my face as I stood in front of my stove. Grabbing tissues to staunch the tears, I was bewildered. Just as raw flesh suddenly exposed to the air causes excruciating pain, so my emotions, suddenly released from captivity, brought me a similar anguish.

On my emotional roller-coaster ride, I rose from feeling sorrow for Janie's problems to the exciting hope of discovering a friend to confide in, then plunged into this inexplicably painful sadness.

My emotions continued to swing all afternoon. I was no longer in control. Janie's words had stirred the dead spot in my heart where my feelings had once lived, and I fell in love with her. After all my efforts to avoid this very problem, that feeling of love for a woman suddenly seized control of my emotions.

I couldn't pretend any longer. I had to get out of my marriage.

Almost five months later, on Friday evening, January 7, 2000, when my husband had finished eating supper and we were both still sitting at the kitchen table, I gathered up all my courage and said, "Jim, I need to talk to you. I'm very unhappy. You've probably sensed this."

"Yes, something's going on with you."

And something was going on with me—ever since my Sunday conversation with Janie. The emotions that had overwhelmed me that afternoon had taken control of my life. I couldn't sleep, had lost my appetite, and was constantly on edge. The only way to regain my sanity was to get out of my marriage. So I replied, "I don't know any other way to say it, but I need to take a sabbatical, a leave from the marriage for a while."

Jim appeared to droop all over. "I'm very, very

sorry to hear this."

"I plan to sleep in the other bedroom and am going to Lubbock after church Sunday and stay in Laura's apartment for a week or two to think through some things."

Laura was twenty-one, a beautiful, intelligent, tender-hearted daughter who was then a senior at Texas Tech University. Five days earlier I'd confided in her, told her I was gay. "Mom," she'd said immediately, "you've got to get a divorce." Every day since then, she'd said, "Mom, you've got to do it. Don't keep putting it off. You've got to get a divorce."

"Do you think that's the only solution?" Jim asked me. "To separate?"

"Yes. You know how many years we've tried to make this work. You'd be much better off if you had somebody you could love."

"I don't want anybody else."

"You'd be happier."

"No. I'd be happier with someone who's—"

"A different person than I am."

"No, let me behind that wall. I've never been able to. This hurts. It cuts to the inner part of my soul because we've always said that, no matter what, we'd make it work, that we're survivors."

"If you can't have some kind of happiness, it's just not worth it."

"Oh, I don't agree. You've worked hard and made me happy. But I evidently haven't put forth enough effort to do the same. Do you think our marriage is absolutely irreparable?"

"Yes."

"Then if you feel that way, you're talking about divorcing!"

"That's probably what will happen."

Jim looked like I'd hit him with an iron skillet. "I've always said that if we ever got a divorce it would be because you left. I tolerated the unhappy parts of the marriage in order to keep the family together. Can you say anything else other than the fact that you're unhappy?"

"No. I don't think I can."

"Well, I've been unhappy for fifteen years!" (When we'd come close to divorcing fifteen years earlier, I'd placed some restrictions on our lovemaking.)

"Then why are we sticking it out? Why don't we try to be happy in other ways, separately? Why both be unhappy?"

"Because I thought we made a commitment."

"We did, and we've stuck with it year after year. But it's getting worse. Okay? It's worse."

"You really think so?"

"Yes. There's a strain in the atmosphere. The children noticed it during Christmas."

"I didn't feel that. But if you've already made up your mind and we can't try to reconcile, then let's just go ahead and get a divorce."

The conversation continued, sometimes touching on hurtful incidents of the past. I was amazed at myself for actually initiating this discussion.

Later, however, I realized how Jim and I harmed our four children by rearing them in a home where their parents didn't love each other. We were polite and considerate to each other—but unaffectionate. I'd avoided touching him, though some nights in bed I'd longed just to be held, nothing else. But this hadn't been possible with him.

Jim expressed his belief that I would never need

anyone else, that I had the capacity to happily live alone. He then ventured closer to the truth than he imagined when he stated, "I can't get inside that private shield of yours. It just rips me apart." After he expressed his love for me, we decided there was nothing else to say.

My heart was heavy as I stood up and walked out of the kitchen and into the guest bedroom. I'd actually asked Jim for a divorce, and he had agreed to it.

I should have felt happy to have at last broken free of a relationship that had transformed me into a disconnected person—detached from who I knew myself to be. I no longer recognized myself. Denying who and what I was, accepting the role of a submissive wife, I'd learned to hate myself. For years I'd felt as if I were walking around as only a shadow of the real me. Sitting down on the bed, I was numb, almost in shock.

Laura came into the bedroom that evening to see how I was doing. As we sat on the bed together and held hands, she said, "Mom, you need to talk to a professional counselor."

Her suggestion hit me at the right time. I'd been telling myself that I needed to talk with someone. My life was in a mess. My sorrow and pain for the past several months had made me feel as if I had only three choices: suicide, a mental institution, or divorce. These three choices had been going through my head constantly. And the divorce was just a stop-gap solution. I knew I needed help.

"I don't know anyone I can talk with," I replied.

"I do, Mom. A psychologist who's a professional counselor taught one of my classes at Texas Tech. He's great. I'll call him right now and make an appointment for you to see him while you're in Lubbock. Okay?"

"Yes," I said. "I'll talk with him if he can see me."

Laura located the doctor's number and called him at home that evening. His schedule was full, but he agreed to work me in for an hour's appointment. This would be a first for me—admitting to someone the pain I was experiencing due to my feelings for Janie. But I was ready. I had to do it, for my own sake.

I slept only a little, still disbelieving that I'd actually asked Jim for a divorce and was now spending the night in another room. I felt relief and guilt, along with the continuing deep pain I'd felt since my life-changing conversation with Janie five months earlier.

The next day I talked with Michael, our thirty-year-old entrepreneur, telling him I'd asked his father for a divorce.

"Have you been planning this all along," he asked, "and were just waiting until Laura finished college?"

"No," I truthfully answered. "I haven't. And it has nothing to do with Laura."

"Mom," he said, "you and Dad are just on different planes—completely unable to communicate. I can say something to Dad and it doesn't bother him at all, but if you say exactly the same thing, it pushes his buttons. You're always pushing his buttons, you know."

"You're right, Michael. That's one of the things I tried to tell your dad last night—that I'd become afraid to talk with him for fear of angering him—that I felt intimidated by him."

As Michael hugged me, he said, "Mom, I just want you to be happy."

Later in the day I visited with our eldest, J.W., our thirty-four-year-old, single, elementary-school teacher. He, too, was very kind, loving, and supportive. He said the same thing as Michael. "Mother, we love you and just want you to be happy."

The following day, I taught my Sunday-school class as usual. Seven members were present—a big group. The number had been growing, which pleased me. I didn't share my personal trauma with these women, but I did inform them I'd be out of town the following Sunday and had already asked one of their favorite substitutes to step in.

As soon as I left church, I drove to Mother's apartment, located in a retirement home. Mother, eighty-nine, was a beloved resident, respected, and a humdinger of a bridge player. Tall and thin, she regularly received compliments on her beautiful white hair. Mother never had any problems speaking her mind or speaking out. I grew up in her shadow and now saw myself very like her. Dad had passed away almost four years earlier, so two years later she'd left her many friends and moved from Little Rock to Tyler, in order to be close to me, her only daughter.

As I entered her living room, I came right to the point. "Mother, I've asked Jim for a divorce, and I'm now on my way to Lubbock for several weeks."

"You're getting a divorce?"

"Yes, I am."

She then amazed me. "I know you've been unhappy for a long time. This doesn't surprise me. I just want you to be happy. When did you say you're going to Lubbock?"

"Now. As soon as I leave here. The car's already packed. I'll be staying in Laura's apartment. You have her phone number. I'll call home tonight to let everyone know I've arrived safely."

I'd dreaded telling her, feeling certain she'd be hurt or embarrassed and try to talk me out of my decision. But that didn't happen.

We said a few more words, hugged, she admonished me to drive carefully, and I left—my heart much lighter. Her reaction pleasantly surprised me, as did everyone else's. I'd braced myself for condemnation that never came.

A little over seven hours later, I arrived in Lubbock, wiped out. After all, I'd been awake since 3:15 that morning, had taught a Sunday-school class, and had then driven 400 miles.

Climbing into bed, I felt a desire to read. I'd brought library books with me on the legal aspects of divorce and the financial decisions that need to be made, as well as some I thought would help me better understand homosexuality and my deep emotional pain.

I chose Mel White's *Stranger at the Gate*. I read, and I cried. This was the first book I'd ever read on homosexuality, and I was then sixty-one. I placed a box of tissues beside me on the bed, and every few minutes I stopped to blow my nose and wipe away tears. For the first time in my life I discovered that other people like me exist, have feelings similar to mine, and have suffered in much the same way.

I'd always believed I was unique, one of a kind, atypical. I cried and cried for the lost years, for all those lonely years of silence and fear. I cried for the years of repression and the unwarranted guilt I carried all my life for something I couldn't help. I discovered other people are like me, people I never knew existed. Never before had I cried like this. A purging was taking place, an emptying. The tears kept coming. After I read a page or two and learned something that applied directly to me, the tears would start again. Reading, sobbing, reading, sobbing. I released repressed emotions and learned I wasn't the terrible sinner I always thought I was. Finally,

I cut off the light and slept a while.

As soon as I awakened, I picked up White's book and continued to read. This time I took time to note page numbers, enabling me to later on summarize the points I considered most important.

White's statements excited me. He wrote, "Doing justice begins by walking away from the churches and the synagogues, the preachers, priests and rabbis, who use God's word to condemn homosexuality and into churches and fellowships where we are loved and respected as God's children who happen to be gay."

Mel White expressed my feelings exactly when he stated, "Feeling abandoned by God, by the church, and by society, I longed to end my life."

"Misusing the Bible to support old prejudice is not a new phenomenon," White wrote as he gave documented examples.

Everything he said hit home. All my life, I'd avoided reading about homosexuality. "By not paying any attention to it, it'll just go away," I'd thought. The only information I'd ever gleaned on the forbidden subject came from either the Ann Landers column or the Dear Abby column. Thank goodness their comments were sensible, without the prejudice I normally heard from Christians and family.

As I took a break from reading that Monday morning, I thought back to the previous day when Janie had lingered for a few minutes after I completed the Sunday-school lesson. She was the only one in the group who knew I'd asked Jim for a divorce, as I'd called her on Saturday to tell her of the events of the night before. She, along with Laura, had been encouraging me to take this step.

I could still hear her saying, "Lou Anne, this is

something you just have to do." Over and over, she'd encouraged me to get out of the marriage. Each time she said it I knew she was right, but doing what is right can sometimes be very, very difficult. After the other class members left, Janie asked, "Are you all right, precious?"

"Yes, I'm fine," I replied, though I was probably still in a state of shock. She then handed me a little gift bag containing a book wrapped in gift paper and tied with a bow. "I want you to read this," she explained. "I didn't think the other members of the class needed to see it so I wrapped it up like a gift. But I had it at the house and thought it would be good for you."

Thanking her for the loan of Bruce Bawer's *A Place At The Table*, I visited with her for a few minutes. "One of the things Jim said to me as we discussed the divorce was that there had always been a wall between us," I told her. "He didn't realize how right he is."

"Lou Anne," she replied, " he knows what it is. He just doesn't want to admit it, but he knows."

I didn't believe it had ever occurred to Jim that I'm gay, yet a part of me wished he did know so I'd never have to explain it to him. Then a wave of fear passed through me. What if he found out before our divorce was final? Would he make the divorce difficult? "I have to continue to guard my secret," I told myself.

After a trip to the grocery store that morning, I climbed back into bed, propped myself up as I snuggled under the covers, and continued to read. I also called Josh, the only son with whom I hadn't talked. Josh would soon be twenty-nine and lived with his wife in the Houston area. He worked for a company that sub-contracted with NASA, involved in preparing experiments taken up in space ships. His comments mirrored what my other children said. "Mom, I just want you to be happy." However, he did add, "I can't help but selfishly wish our baby could have the same family togetherness that I had as a child."

I thought this a very strange statement, as the family togetherness he'd experienced as a child was a pretend closeness between his parents. But then I reminded myself that he could have been referring to visiting his grandparents in Little Rock. He had enjoyed being a part of that happy, extended family, and he wanted his children to have a similar opportunity.

Chapter Nine

On Wednesday, I met with Dr. Kerns. After arriving at his office, I had to complete a long questionnaire. When I read, "Tell me in what way you think I will be able to help you," I wrote, "Frankly, I don't think you can."

Dr. Kerns read my statement and laughed. "You really don't think I can help you?"

"That's right. No one can do anything for me." My problems, in my mind, were insurmountable, unsolvable. I kept the appointment so I could bare my soul, and that's exactly what I did that afternoon.

I confided exactly why I married Jim and how miserable that decision had made me for so many years. Although I despised the person I'd become, I was very proud of my children and showed Dr. Kerns a picture of the six of us. I told him everything—my pain and misery, the reason for it, and the hopelessness of my situation. I mentioned Jim's extreme prejudice against homosexuality, of hearing him, as a high-school principal, say that he would never allow homosexuals to teach in his school because they had no business being around children. He had no idea a homosexual was mothering his four children. His attitude made it impossible for me to be open with him.

"Do you think he might have a good attitude if you explained to him 'the wall' that's between the two of you?" he asked.

"No. No way in the world."

As I poured out my heart to him that afternoon, I cried continually. A dam had broken, one that had been well fortified for the past forty years, and my anguish was pouring out. He placed a box of tissues next to me as I sobbed for most of the hour, gut-wrenching cries of hopelessness. Several times he became so concerned about me that he left his chair to sit beside me, patting me on the back. Several times he asked, "Do you believe God loves you despite your homosexuality?"

"Yes," I sobbed. "I know He loves me, but I don't know why He made me this way."

"If Jesus walked into this room right now, do you believe He would put His arms around you and tell you how much He loves you?"

"Yes," I admitted. "But I don't understand this heartbreak. I don't understand why I'm hurting so many people. Why I will have to endure the disapproval of others. None of it makes any sense unless...unless God has always had a plan for me to use my life experiences to help someone else. That thought is all that keeps me going."

"You do have difficult times ahead of you," he said. "But you don't have to place an ad in the paper about your situation.

"You need to make some definite plans prior to returning to Tyler," he suggested. "Be specific. Decide before you leave here where you'll spend the night, where you'll eat your meals, whom you will see, and whether you will attend church. Make these decisions ahead of time."

When our session was over and I stood up to go, Dr. Kerns said, "I don't normally do this, but would you mind if I pray?"

"No, of course not," I answered.

Dr. Kerns held my hands as he asked God to watch over me and send comfort to me. At no time during the session did he even question my decision to get a divorce.

ॐॐॐॐॐ

Although I didn't turn out my light until eleven p.m., I was wide-awake the next morning by five, probably four thirty. I decided to splurge and eat breakfast at IHOP. My weight had dropped, and I didn't need to lose any more pounds.

I entered the doors of IHOP at five thirty and received wonderful service so early in the day. The food was good, but I had little appetite. I ate almost half of an omelet and a small biscuit, and drank half a glass of orange juice.

When I couldn't push any more down, I paid my bill, got in my car, and drove the loop around Lubbock. I set the speed control, listened to Beethoven's Piano Concerto #1 in C Major, and drove a practically empty highway lit by streetlights and a sprinkling of stars in a dark sky. It took twenty-four minutes to circle the city. When I returned to Laura's apartment, I climbed back in bed, feeling headachy. I must have slept for a little while.

After supper, I called Mother. I'd been feeling guilty about not communicating with her and tried to keep the conversation upbeat to hide how depressed I was. At one point, she said, "I woke up before five this morning thinking about Jeff Tatum."

"What in the world made you think of him?"

Mother's answer amazed me. "I figure he's probably the one you've been thinking of, the reason you've decided to leave Jim."

"Oh, Mother! I can't believe you said that."

"Isn't he the one who drove out to Big Spring to give you a big diamond ring?"

"He offered me a diamond ring while we were at Baylor. You must be thinking of Allen Adair. He drove up from South Texas to Big Spring to see me."

"Yes, I remember him. He gave you that pretty sweater from Germany. I remember all those fellows, but I'm sure I wouldn't recognize them if I saw them."

"You probably wouldn't recognize Duane Morris. I went steady with him my senior year in high school. Remember Duane?"

"He used to work at that restaurant in Austin."

"Yes, the Nighthawk. That's the one. He worked in both their restaurants, the one on the south side as well as the one on the north side. He used to be tall and skinny, but now he's a big man. He owned a car dealership in Austin. He and his wife, Wendy, own a ranch, close to Kyle, I think. His wife and I used to be in the same Sunday-school class at Hyde Park Baptist in Austin."

"Well, I figure it's one of those fellows you're thinking about."

"Mother, you're wasting your time. Quit thinking. And that's all I'm going to say on the subject. You're worrying about something that's not happening."

"Oh, I'm not worrying about it. It's not my problem."

❧❧❧❧

I awoke Friday morning at 3:35 recalling the questionnaire I'd completed at Dr. Kerns's office. Listed at the bottom of the questionnaire, in rather small print, were perhaps up to a hundred various problems I might be experiencing. I circled quite a few: sadness, marriage, suicide, depression, sexual problems, and sleep disorders. I then marked the two most important problems: depression and marriage.

At some point during the interview, after I'd expressed my long-standing desire to die and the many, many times I considered killing myself, Dr. Kerns asked, "Why didn't you ever commit suicide?"

"Because of the children," I replied. "I knew they needed me. It would be so unfair to them, and to my parents."

At that point, we discussed my homosexuality and the fact that, because Dr. Kerns works for a Christian counseling service, he's had little contact with my particular problem. We spent a few minutes discussing it in very general terms, and then I said, "That's where the hate comes from, you know. From Christians."

"Yes, you're right," he said.

His affirmation validated my belief that religion/ churches are the root of prejudice against gays.

❧❧❧❧❧

Mother called again that night. "I think I've figured out who you're interested in," she said immediately. "When you asked for that good-smelling hand lotion for a birthday gift, I decided I knew then who it was."

My heart began to pound, because the hand lotion had a direct bearing on Janie. The scent was her scent. Fear set in. I didn't say a thing, and she continued. "It's Frank Smitherman, isn't it?"

I laughed with relief, along with the ridiculousness of her conclusion. Frank and I had taught together, shared a classroom for several years. We supported each other in that environment, were certainly friends, but our relationship never went beyond that. Besides, he was at least fifteen years younger than I, maybe twenty. "Mother," I said, "your imagination's working overtime. I can't believe what you're doing. I'm not interested in Frank Smitherman, for goodness sakes!"

"It dawned on me that when you asked for that expensive hand lotion, you were up to something. If it's not Frank, then it must be someone at the church."

"Why would you think that?"

"Because you're always going to the church for meetings."

"You're wasting your time, Mother. I told you that last night, and I'm telling you again right now. Quit thinking! It's not going to get you anywhere. I'm not interested in anyone."

"Well, I figured you want to be free to be with someone else."

"I don't have someone waiting for me. There's no one."

We talked a while longer, about the children and her new hairdresser. I closed the conversation by saying, "I can hardly wait for your next phone call to see who in the world you've thought of next."

Several hours passed, and the more I thought about mother's meddling questions, the angrier I became. Memories flooded back from my teenage years of when she put me through the third degree after every date. "Where did you go? Who was with you? Did you kiss?" Oh, how I hated her questions. I dreaded walking into the house after a date, knowing I'd have to endure her inquisition. What right did she have to ask me such questions? The nerve!

Chapter Ten

Jim called while I was still in Lubbock and couldn't have been nicer—no pleading for me to change my mind. None.

"I'd like for us to keep everything friendly," he said. "You're welcome to stay at the house until you find a place to live. I want us to go over the financial details of the divorce. We don't need to get involved with lawyers. The two of us can work everything out in a friendly way."

I told him that I agreed and would like for both of us to be able to maintain the standard of living we were used to.

He even offered to continue to take care of my car for me in exchange for a few home-cooked meals. He also wanted me to be in the same house with him when Josh and Sandy and their baby came to visit.

I thought this a rather odd scenario but was delighted to hear Jim being so nice and friendly, so I quickly agreed. "I'll be glad to come over and cook for all of us."

His desire to have all of us together for visits made me realize the divorce would be easier than I'd expected. I also felt his plans for family gatherings would be short-lived because once he became interested in someone else, he certainly wouldn't be inviting me over. I told myself, "We'll cross that bridge when we come to it."

❁❁❁❁

I returned home from Lubbock with some type of virus and stayed in bed for almost a week. Then I located a small apartment in a gated community for seniors for only $470 a month. I was delighted to have found a place so quickly and easily, as my strength was gone.

I regularly asked myself during this time, "What do I think I'm doing, getting a divorce, making a mess of my life at age sixty-one? I'm giving up everything I know and stepping out into an unknown world as a single person. A divorcée, for goodness sakes! Me! Do I really want to do this?"

The answer that quickly resounded in my mind was, "What's the alternative? Do I want to stay married for the rest of my life?"

"No," I told myself. "That's an impossible situation. I cannot, absolutely cannot, stay married. I have no choice. I must get a divorce."

"Will getting a divorce solve my problem of being in love with Janie? Make me happy?"

"No. It won't solve that problem. My misery will continue. But getting a divorce will help."

❁❁❁❁

On January 31, 2000, Jim and I agreed on how to divide the money. I was satisfied that I could live on the smaller portion I'd asked for. I wanted to show Jim he'd have enough to continue the house payments and maintain his standard of living. We'd always lived on a strict budget, which I'd drawn up. I therefore prepared Jim's budget for February—something he could use to understand how his portion of the money would meet his needs.

The budget was my responsibility because I enjoyed it. Jim abided by it, but he didn't enjoy managing money. He never complained, however, because we were spending and saving his income wisely, and I believe he was thankful I was careful with it. But finances were my forte, and I even completed our yearly tax returns. The divorce would force Jim at age sixty-six into financial areas new to him, and I hated to leave him unprepared. I promised to balance his checkbook at the end of February, then took time to show him some basic steps before I headed to a bank to open an account in my name.

Jim called a lawyer to check on the cost of handling the divorce: $400 plus a $150 filing fee. We agreed to split the cost. Even if we filed right away, it would be April before the divorce was final.

❧❧❧❧

I moved out of our home to my small apartment the following day. Having been ill for almost two weeks, I decided to take only a few bare essentials, to get partially settled, and to pick up additional items from the house in the next few days. Jim was helpful, and we both worked hard all day. As he assembled the bed for me in my apartment, I silently said, "Thank you, God" for Jim's willingness to help and his generous attitude. We completed the last load after dark, and when I made no move to get back in the car with him, he said, "You are coming back to the house to sleep, aren't you?"

"No, I plan to stay here."

"But you don't have anything set up."

"The bed's put together. That's all I need. I can

find some sheets to put on it. I'll be all right. Really. I want to stay here tonight."

Reluctantly, Jim left me alone in the apartment. Later, after nine p.m., I drove to Walmart to purchase shelf paper and a few food items.

Jim and our thirty-year-old son, Michael, both called to check on me the following day. I stayed very busy putting things away. I read that day that "The most powerful yearning is for a past one never had." This insight described my feelings exactly.

During my long marriage I had constantly yearned for a life I denied myself when I was twenty—and always wished for something I could never have.

≈⁂≈

After spending ten days making my apartment livable, for the first time in weeks, I experienced an overwhelming sadness. Tears were ready to fall constantly. I wasn't certain what caused this: perhaps going through a box of old letters and notes—many written to thank me or praise me for something or another. (Aren't those the letters people save—the uplifting ones?)

Many were from Barbara Lawrence, a friend from church who was a year or two older than I. Barbara's intelligence amazed me, and I admired the way she always seemed to know what was going on in the church. Her father, now deceased, had been pastor of a large Baptist church in a neighboring town, so she was well grounded in scripture, and everyone regarded her as an excellent Sunday-school teacher.

Her numerous contacts with me emphasized the tremendous effort she'd exerted to be my friend—yet

I did so little for her in return. Guilt crept over me. I'd treated her rather shabbily, and I knew why. I was abiding by my old promise to myself to never again have a close friend.

I looked at the evidence of Barbara's perseverance— notes, gifts of books, help with Sunday-school lessons, invitations to lunch, and written encouragement. She was always there for me, willing to be my friend.

An overpowering urge came over me to unburden myself to her. How strange that I should even consider such a thing, yet I felt a need to explain my aloofness, my pulling away from her offers of friendship. I imagined her reaction when she heard of my sexual orientation and could picture her as totally amazed, perhaps repulsed, or maybe just smiling as she said something like, "I kinda figured that." Who knew how she would react? I felt an uncomfortable churning deep inside, of not just my stomach, but of my spirit. My whole being was sad.

≈≈≈≈≈

I enjoyed my little apartment, especially the freedom to do what I wanted when I wanted. More than that, I was able to relax, knowing I no longer needed to weigh my words before I spoke. Yes, I got lonely. But I'd always been lonely, even around people. I continued to live in a fantasy world, thinking about Janie, a person I had no right to yearn for. It was getting worse. I felt as if I were digging my own grave in this regard. It made no sense that I was so completely infatuated with an individual so very different from me. I dreamed of our being together, just day-after-day being together. I realized that the emotions, the longings I felt were worse when we were apart. Sometimes I thought I'd just explode! That's when the tears came.

I reminded myself it was just an infatuation. But knowing this to be true didn't lessen the pain. I was too old to be feeling this type of emotion. I was like a teenager with my first crush. The pain was indescribable, unbelievable, incredible, and devastating as it developed within me a terrible feeling of hopelessness that pervaded me with despair. Yes, hopelessness, because there was no chance of my fantasy coming true. The person I loved was off limits, in the same way a parish priest would be off limits. That type of love was wrong, sinful. But I continued to live in my fantasy world where the two of us were always together.

The next morning I awoke at three thirty and couldn't go back to sleep, so I finally got up at six. My weight was still dropping, and from a previous high of 132, I was now down to 110 pounds. I'd lost my appetite, my emotional state affecting my physical condition.

Chapter Eleven

I'll always remember February 28 because of an email Jim sent me late the previous evening and the decision I made when answering it. He expressed anger and resentment that his world had been turned upside down without his understanding why. "To help me reach some sort of mental and emotional closure, I really need to know specifically why this is happening. Would you do me the courtesy of sharing with me specific things over the last several years (or last 37 years) that have caused you to ask for a divorce."

When I finished reading it, I said to myself, "I have to tell him the truth. It's not fair to keep him in the dark. He's hurting as badly as I am—in a different way, of course, but he's still hurting. It would be cruel to withhold the truth from him."

But even as I had these thoughts, other thoughts began to take over. "He won't want to hear what I need to tell him. The truth may infuriate him so much he may delay the divorce or cause problems with the division of money." With those thoughts in mind, I asked myself if I should wait until the divorce was final to be truthful with him.

It wouldn't be final for almost six weeks. All day I agonized about answering his letter and finally concluded that I couldn't wait that long. I felt that if he knew the truth and that I accepted responsibility for the problems in our marriage, he would gain some type of relief.

Late that evening, I sat at my computer and wrote Jim a long, detailed e-mail, including some quotes from Mel White.

I don't fit your stereotype of a homosexual. That's because the only ones you hear about are the oddballs. The rest of us are so afraid to come out of the closet that no one knows who we are. We're the teachers, lawyers, doctors, business people that you interact with day after day and never dream that we are gay. We are rich and poor, young and old, parents and grandparents, children and grandchildren. We come from every possible race, religious, and ethnic background. We're not a menace to the country. Quite the contrary, we are a powerful, loving, gifted, creative presence.

Most people who condemn homosexuals are not wicked. More often, they're uninformed. Not unintelligent—on the contrary...they are often very intelligent—but uninformed.

At the end of my e-mail, I gave Jim permission to talk with friends and our pastor about what I had said. I told him I was so tired of living a lie that I was almost anxious for it to all come out.

I clicked the send button and the die was cast. The secret I'd protected all my life was no longer a secret. My life was changing, and I wasn't certain what was about to happen. All I knew was that my heart felt lighter and was no longer bound by that all-encompassing vise-grip of fear.

A second e-mail from Jim quickly arrived. He said he'd always suspected this might be the problem and wanted to come by and visit the next day, that he still loved me.

✦✦✦✦

When Jim arrived early the next morning, he took me in his arms, held me tight, and began sobbing. I held him and cried. When we eventually sat down, I placed a box of tissues between us on the sofa. I answered whatever questions he had, allowing him to vent his heartbreak caused by his never being able to get close to me.

Having given Jim permission to tell others, I knew the news would probably spread rapidly. I decided to send Laura and Barbara Lawrence copies of both Jim's letter to me as well as my reply to him. Barbara was bound to hear about this from someone in the church. She'd been too nice to me to allow her to be broadsided by the news, so I wanted to warn her.

Along with the letters, I sent this explanation.

Barbara, I've spent my life trying not to have a close friend—always fearful I'd feel something toward her I shouldn't. I've done little to encourage our friendship, and that's why.

Right now I'm concerned about Janie Robbins because we've developed a close friendship. When my sexual orientation becomes public knowledge, I'm afraid people will assume things about Janie that just aren't true. Though I've warned her not to publicly acknowledge our friendship, she keeps telling me she's not worried. I haven't worried so much about you. I figure you can handle it.

If you have questions, or want to talk, that's fine. If not, I certainly understand. No problem.

Lou Anne

❧ ❧ ❧ ❧

Jim called the next day, asking if he could come over again.

"Sure," I told him.

As we sat together on the sofa, Jim told me about his conversation the night before with our son Michael.

"He had a tough time accepting your news," Jim said. "He knows you're a good mother, a good cook and all that, and he still loves you very much, but he just doesn't understand."

"Please get Mel White's book, *Stranger at the Gate*," I urged him. "I want both of you to read it. I really think it'll help you understand what's happening."

"Michael's concerned about all of this being known. He asked me some very pointed questions last night. Questions that made me stop and think. He said, 'Why do you want everyone to know about this, Dad? This is a family matter.'"

"Don't tell anyone for *my* sake!" I said.

Jim said he'd probably unburden himself to a few close friends, and I let him know that I wanted to be the one to tell my mother. I suspected that deep down she'd known the truth for a long time and hoped she felt guilty when I told her.

"She never hurt you on purpose," Jim said.

"I know that. She just did what her society and her religion demanded. But I want to tell her. I owe her that."

Jim then said he planned to inform our son in Houston, and it bothered me somewhat that he was the one telling the children, but I kept quiet.

Then he surprised me by asking, "Did you think about your sexual orientation every year during our marriage?"

"Every year? It was more like every day!"

"It must have been a miserable life."

How true, I thought, but I didn't say a word.

When he stood up ready to leave, he put his arms around me and kissed me. "This is something I want the kids to see," he said.

I meekly replied, "Okay," not knowing what else to do at that point.

❧ ❧ ❧ ❧

Later in the day, I listened to a phone message from Gwen Patterson, who works with me on the task force involved in organizing a local Christian Women's Job Corps to train and further educate women presently on welfare. This type of organization is dear to my heart—helping those who really need it and doing so in a way that doesn't involve a monetary handout but a training program. Gwen, aware of my divorce, invited me to join her for dinner.

Calling her back, I said, "Gwen, I'm just not up to meeting in a public place."

"Would you like to talk about it?"

"Not over the phone. I'm not certain it's something you want to hear. I'll just explain it by e-mail. Then, if you still want to talk, give me a call."

"Lou Anne, please be assured that I'm your friend," she said.

"You might not be after you read what I plan to send you. I'll just wait to see if I hear from you."

❧❧❧❧

My emotions were so raw. For days, I was sleep deprived and constantly full of turmoil. I kept telling myself, "Keep your head on straight, girl. Don't lose it."

Laura called one afternoon. "Hi, Mom. Just called to see how you're doing. Now, be truthful."

"It's been pretty rough, sweetie." I explained that I'd told her dad. "Now others are finding out that I'm different, and I don't know from one day to the next who's heard and who hasn't. I'm afraid my emotions aren't holding up very well."

Laura began crying, and I assumed she was feeling sadness for herself and the upheaval in her life—her mother moving out of the house, her parents divorcing, and now others finding out she has a gay mother. That would upset anyone. "Are you going to be all right?" I asked. "I'm so sorry you have to go through all this."

"Mother, I'm crying because of *you*! I'm so *worried* about you. Are *you* going to be all right?"

"I'll be fine, dear. It's a little rough right now, but I'll make it." I let her know that she could share any of this with her friends if she needed to talk to someone. "I'm through trying to keep all this a secret."

❧❧❧❧

Late that afternoon, the e-mail arrived from Barbara that I'd anxiously been waiting for all day. I trembled with fear and excitement as I read it.

She assured me that she loved me, that she'd suspected I was gay but didn't want to risk our friendship by asking.

I value you for the person you are, and I grieve for the pain you've endured and for the rough time I'm sure you still have ahead of you. I can't imagine not being friends with you for any reason other than if you choose not to. I'd love to talk to you some time, any time—and I'll probably ask you more questions that are none of my business.

She said I didn't have to answer her questions but that it was rather hard for her to understand how I felt, just as she'd never been able to put herself in the shoes of someone who wanted to climb mountains or travel into space.

I can't imagine your being asked to leave the church, although if you find someone with whom you want to have a relationship I can imagine it getting rather uncomfortable for you there. I'm your friend, always have been, always have thought we have much in common. I'd love to see you any time. Call me!

She also suggested that I send our pastor some of my recent correspondence with Jim regarding our divorce, so he could read it quietly.

As soon as I received her e-mail, relief and joy flooded me, and I glimpsed the terrific friendship she was offering me. I replied immediately.

Thank you. What else is there to say? You amaze me. I do want to talk, but I'm not ready to handle this subject in a public place. Maybe you can come here or I can visit in your place.

I also told her that I didn't know our pastor well

enough to approach him in any way and that the idea of doing so threw me.

You're one in a million, Barbara—a special gift from God. Want to come over Thursday or Friday?

Barbara responded in just a few minutes.

I'm free both days—tomorrow, too, but I think I need a down day for my brain to return to Texas time after our overseas trip.

She went on to explain that it was probably best for our pastor to know the facts from me instead of from Jim or someone else, and that an e-mail might be the easiest way for me to communicate with him.

However, I still wasn't sure I wanted to take that step just yet, though after I reconsidered the situation, I followed her advice.

❧ ❧ ❧ ❧

In the middle of these e-mails back and forth with Barbara, Gwen Patterson with the Christian Women's Job Corps called and asked if she could drop by for a visit. She arrived soon afterward.

I'd sent her the e-mails between Jim and me that outed me. She was one of the most fundamental, legalistic Christians I'd talk to about my sexual orientation, so I shared more of my past with her than I had with anyone else. I wanted to see her reaction, to learn how bad it might be for me.

Gwen stayed for an hour and a half. I wanted her to realize I hadn't chosen this sexual preference, as most fundamentalist Christians believe. I wanted her to be aware of the frustration I'd experienced in dealing with prejudice and bigotry, and the lifelong decisions that gays make by marrying because it's expected of them. I wanted to stun Gwen by describing the agony of thirty-seven years of unnatural heterosexual sex from a homosexual's viewpoint.

I also took time to relate an incident that had occurred in one of the meetings of our task force. About eight members, prior to the beginning of the meeting, had begun talking about *Angels in America*, a controversial play to be performed at nearby Kilgore College. Negative opinions about this play abounded throughout East Texas, and a form of political blackmail resulted when the Gregg County commissioners rescinded $50,000 that supported the college's yearly Texas Shakespeare Festival in retaliation for hosting the play.

The play centered on homosexuals, and that evening nearly all of these task-force members began venting blatant prejudice toward homosexuals. Dumbfounded, I'd sat there not moving, not saying a word. I'd wanted to get up and walk out of the room, but I didn't. I wished I'd had the nerve to say, "I find this talk very offensive." But I just sat there, silent. I was the secretary, and they depended on me to take the notes. So I listened to so-called Christians voicing horribly prejudicial statements as they advocated banning the play.

While visiting with Gwen, I said, "What I heard that night was obscene bigotry." Then I added, "I'm not certain I can fit into a group like that."

"I just don't know what to say," Gwen stated.

"I understand completely. Don't worry about it."

"I hope you're not still battling suicidal thoughts."

"No, I'm not, and I haven't since I asked for a divorce almost two months ago."

"I still want to be your friend, Lou Anne. Feel free to call me any time."

"Thanks, Gwen. I appreciate that."

"Would it be all right if I pray for you?"

"That would be wonderful. Of course you can."

And Gwen prayed a beautiful prayer. She's truly gifted in that area, as her petitions to God rolled off her lips in almost a poetic form. I only hoped she would be as willing to listen to God with the same fervency as she prayed.

Chapter Twelve

Jim wanted to tell our three boys about my sexual orientation, but I wanted to be the one to break the news to Josh and his wife. That way Jim would have told two of our children, and I would have spoken to two. That sounded fair to me.

I sent the "two letters" to Josh because it seemed the best way to explain it all. My e-mail explained why I decided to come out and gave the recipients privacy as they read and tried to assimilate the position in which they were placed. Also, I didn't have to sit and watch their reactions, which might not be positive at the outset but hopefully would improve as the shock wore off.

Next I e-mailed Jim to apprise him of those I'd told—Barbara, our pastor, Gwen Patterson, and Josh and Sandy. I also let him know that I hadn't told Mother, but whenever I did, I'd inform him.

I was aware it would probably upset him that I'd told Josh, because he'd planned to drive to Houston to do that in person. Although I normally avoided angering Jim whenever possible, I just didn't care what his reaction might be in this regard.

❧ ❧ ❧ ❧ ❧

That afternoon, I received a response from my pastor, Bob Watson, who said that my e-mail had moved him to tears. He wrote that he was relieved to receive my letter and appreciated my entrusting such heartfelt matters to him.

> *I trust you know they will remain in confidence.*
> *I want you to know that you matter to me.*
> *If you need to talk or even just vent, please don't hesitate to do so. I realize that the issue of sexual preference is such an emotional, misunderstood and volatile subject. I do hope and pray that we can be the church for you in this time, in the best sense of the word. To that end, pray diligently and lean on brothers and sisters-in-Christ like Janie and Barbara, not to mention others, including me. Please know of my thoughts and prayers.*
> *Your brother in Christ,*
> *Bob Watson*

I rejoiced in this letter from my pastor—to think that reading what I had sent him had moved him to tears. Few Baptist pastors would have passed up the opportunity to condemn me for what they perceived as a chosen sexual orientation. The fact that Bob hadn't condemned me made me feel truly blessed to have him for my pastor.

☙ ☙ ☜ ☜

A little later in the day, I received an e-mail from my eldest son, J.W., who teaches elementary school and supplements his teacher's salary by driving a school bus every morning and afternoon.

> *Yesterday as I was arriving at the bus barn, Dad called my cellular and said that he needed to come over to the house later and talk with me. When I got to the*

house (and saw what a mess it was in!), I called him back to suggest that I drive over there, but he was insistent. "You'll understand when I get there," he said.

Boy, that put my mind to wondering. First, I decided he was having a giant garage sale and selling everything out of the house (and the house) and was preparing to move somewhere far away. The other scenario was that he'd already found someone, and she was already living at the house.

I'm glad that you had the courage to be so honest with him and with all of us. Now I'll admit the idea that my mother is gay may take a while to get used to. But it really doesn't change anything about how I feel about you. You're still the same mother I've loved for thirty-four years. To me, the divorce brings more changes to my life (no more family dinners at the house) than news of your sexual orientation does.

I hope and pray that people will be loving and accept you as you are.

I love you, and that's never going to change.

I immediately replied.

Thanks, J.W.

I love you so very much. Surely you know that. Whenever I talk about you, I refer to you as my missionary son. God has used you in so many precious ways. You are special to me, and your letter reaffirms what I already knew about you. Again, thanks so much. I needed that.

Love, Mother

Coming out to my family and close friends kept my emotions at a high pitch. I cried at the least little thing and constantly fought depression and loss of appetite. Josh's sweet wife, Sandy, called and visited with me by phone for almost an hour. Despite the fact she was extremely kind, loving, and non-condemning, I kept crying off and on throughout the conversation.

"Mom," she asked, "I want you to talk Josh out of driving to Tyler tomorrow (260-plus miles). Your news has hit him rather hard, and he feels he needs to talk with you personally. He's in such an emotional state, I don't want him making that long four-hour drive."

"Put him on the phone," I replied, then proceeded to quash his plans by promising to make the drive myself tomorrow afternoon after my visit with Barbara.

After getting off the phone with Sandy, I shared with Barbara, via e-mail, copies of J.W.'s sweet note as well as our pastor's reply to my communication with him.

She replied with this note.

Big surprise—your son loves you, and your pastor recognizes your courage and care! I trust you recognize that as whatever you'd call the keyboarding equivalent of tongue in cheek—thumb in palm?

Bob's caring response and J.W.'s loving one don't surprise me in the slightest. It's not that you've actually changed, Lou Anne. It's just that you're letting us know you better.

❧❧❧❧

When Barbara opened the door for me that morning, my tears immediately began to fall. For two and a half hours, I explained who and what I was, confessing to feelings and relationships I'd previously kept to myself. Barbara brought out my innermost feelings because she was gutsy enough to ask the questions and intelligent enough to know what questions to ask.

I confessed it all, my first crush on a girl in high school, my falling in love when attending Baylor, and the accompanying two-and-a-half-year affair Karen and I carried on in our dorm room.

After I finished my story about Karen, Barbara asked, "Did you ever see her again?"

"Yes, several years later, but we were surrounded by others and restricted to a public conversation. We never had an opportunity to really talk."

"Where is she now?"

"I have no idea. The man she married, Louis Vanmeter, is from British ancestors who settled in South Africa, then moved to Israel. So I don't know what country she's living in. I don't even know if she's still living or how many children she has. Her firstborn was a boy, born a year and a half after my firstborn, and I've heard his name. But she and I broke off contact a long time ago."

"Why?"

"For about twelve years, we corresponded on a fairly regular basis. Then, in 1971, I was especially unhappy in my marriage and wrote her some things I shouldn't have. Our letters were always generic, so we could show anyone. I usually shared her letters with Jim, and she did the same with her husband, Louis. Yet in this particular letter I bemoaned how unhappy I was in my marriage and concluded by saying, 'I'm glad that I at least was able to know what love really is.' I realized after I mailed the letter I shouldn't have said that. How would she explain it to Louis?

"I never received a reply and decided not to write again. Karen evidently had a happy marriage. I was pleased for her, glad she was happy. My letter could have caused problems in her marriage, and I regretted making things tough for her.

"But I miss her, Barbara. I've always missed her. When I'm in a crowd of people, I often look around, thinking that just maybe I'll see her. I sometimes dream of our being together. Just the other night I dreamed we were meeting on a public street, yet we greeted each other by hugging, kissing, and holding each other close, oblivious to passers-by. When I awoke, I thought, 'We never showed any affection toward each other when others were around. We didn't even do what female friends normally do—hug or kiss each other on the cheek.' No, we never touched each other. We were very careful not to. So to have a dream in which we were publicly affectionate seemed strange. It also told me how much I continue to miss her, even after forty years."

"Is there someone else in your life now?" Barbara asked, catching me by surprise.

Tears started again, and I didn't answer.

"You don't want to talk about it, do you?"

"No," I mumbled as I shook my head.

So we went to another subject for a few minutes, and then Barbara surprised me again by asking, "It's Janie, isn't it? You're in love with Janie, aren't you?"

I'd never intended to tell anyone this horrible secret. But Barbara had guessed it, and as I sobbed anew, the answer was obvious.

"If I were you, I'd be in love with Janie, too."

Barbara was so kind—this woman who had been born and bred Baptist, whose father was a Baptist minister—so kind to me. Of all the things I expected to come from her mouth, from any and all Baptists' mouths—condemnation and judgment—Barbara showed loving friendship toward me. How truly fortunate I felt. How blessed to have a friend like her.

"I know I shouldn't be in love with Janie," I said. "I don't want to. It's wrong. I know it's wrong. She's happily married. She's heterosexual. I'll never touch her, never."

"Does she know you're in love with her?"

"Oh, no! I don't want her to ever know. It would kill me if she found out. It's terrible, my being in love with her. I've never been so miserable."

I started to sob again. "All my life I did everything right just to keep something like this from happening. After Karen, I never again allowed myself to have a close friend. I've been so lonely, but I was so terribly afraid I might fall in love with a friend. I avoided physical contact with women. Even with Janie, I did nothing wrong. Not a thing. I don't know why this happened to me. It's so unfair. If I'd done something wrong, then I'd be getting what I deserve, but I didn't. It just happened. It was as if someone were standing behind me with a wooden two by four and just slammed it into my head with all their strength. It just hit me out of the blue. I was standing in the kitchen on a Sunday afternoon, and wham! I started having these terrible thoughts about Janie. I didn't do anything wrong. It just happened." I was wailing.

Barbara moved close to help comfort me. I was in agony admitting such an unforgivable weakness and ashamed for having fallen in love with Janie. Terribly ashamed.

After a few minutes, Barbara suggested, "You need to give up teaching your Sunday-school class, at least for a few months."

"I just can't do that."

"Why not?"

"I have to be able to see Janie every once in a while. I couldn't stand it if I didn't."

"Lou Anne, you've got to quit teaching that class. It doesn't have to be a permanent change. I'm teaching a class on that same floor, some younger ladies I think you'd enjoy being with. Come visit our class."

"No, I can't." But her suggestion did make me think about it. I decided to teach the class this coming Sunday and then just see how things went.

By the time I left Barbara's, I still had a four-hour drive ahead of me. Worried about my safety and well-being, Barbara stated, "I don't think you need to get on the highway at this time. Wait and make the drive another day."

"I'm all right, Barbara. Really I am. I'll play some music and be just fine."

"I don't think you're 'just fine' at all. I don't want you to make this drive."

"I promised I'd go. Josh and Sandy are expecting me."

"If you're intent on going, then come pick out some books on tape. I have quite a collection, and you're welcome to any of them."

I accepted her offer and selected four or five, told Barbara good-bye, and drove away. The book I listened to as I drove to Houston that afternoon was Janet Fitch's *White Oleander*. The story completely escapes me now, but I recall something in it about suicide because I told myself, "You don't need to be listening to this tape right now."

But I listened to all of it and thankfully arrived safely at Josh and Sandy's house, where I spent two emotional nights.

Chapter Thirteen

Sandy and I had some long conversations in which I shared some of the same things I'd shared with Barbara. Sandy is a wonderful wife to Josh, intelligent, hard working, and loving. She's an inch or two taller than Josh, but that doesn't bother them. Josh is so proud of her. Sandy listened, asked a few questions, and made me feel loved and accepted. I'm so fortunate to have her.

That evening, Josh and I went out to dinner. Sandy thought we needed some time together because Josh was finding it difficult to come to grips with having a homosexual mother. Our conversation drained me. When Josh is convinced of something, it's practically impossible to argue with him. Not only does he possess a logical, well-ordered mind, but his college degree is in biomedical engineering. He therefore has more than a smattering of knowledge about the body, including genes, and is convinced people couldn't possibly be born with a different sexual orientation. "All behavior is learned," he stated.

"Josh, we aren't talking about behavior because there's been no 'behavior' on my part since I was in college. This is the way I am, the way I feel. Me! I've tried all my life to change, but I just can't."

"But Mom, something has caused you to be this way. Environment, perhaps. But you can't convince me a person is born this way."

"Josh, all I know is what I am, what I've experienced. I'm positive this isn't something I chose. No fool would choose to be homosexual. That's the most ridiculous supposition I can imagine. Just think about that for a minute."

"Are you trying to tell me the baby we're expecting in July could be gay?"

"Yes, and SO WHAT!" I was feeling frustrated because I had no facts with which to support my position, and even if I had, I couldn't have held my own against Josh. His brilliance has always amazed me. Angry at myself for being so impotent in our argument and angry at Josh for his persistent logic, I said, "If your baby turns out to be gay, you'll treat it just like you would if he wasn't gay. Just love him or her and accept it the way it is without making it feel guilty!"

By then, Josh was becoming upset. "Well, I can't accept that. I can't believe our child could be gay."

"I hope it's not, Josh. But if it is, just love it. That's all. Just love it."

I wish someone had given my parents that advice.

❧❧❧❧

When I returned home to Tyler, I checked my e-mail messages and read one from Gwen Patterson with the Christian women's group.

I've really been thinking about you and praying for you. Your pain is so beyond my abilities to address, that right now, all I can do is pray. You are a very dear person, and I value you and your friendship. I was thinking about our conversation Tuesday and realized that I really never answered your question about coming to the task-force meetings.

At this time, I don't see wisdom in your participation. I doubt this is a surprise, and considering the conversations of the members concerning the homosexual play in Kilgore, I'm afraid you'd feel uncomfortable. I can't speak for the others, but if you're not comfortable, others in the group might not be also.

Lou Anne, I don't want our friendship to end. I do need to ask you to bear with me while I pray for guidance. Can we walk as friends?

Blessings,
Gwen

Now that I'd come out of the closet, I was no longer welcome as a member of the task force for this group. That's the way I took her letter. I sent her a quick reply.

Gwen, yes, we will remain friends. I appreciate your caring attitude and your honesty. I'm not surprised. I'd already decided that was how you felt and perhaps also how I felt. No problem there at all. We can always talk as friends. Whatever questions you have, I will try to answer.

Lou Anne

I shared Gwen's letter with Barbara, who wrote back.

It's good that the friend from the Christian women's group is still a friend, more for her good than for yours. Ultimately you're going to be okay, though you've just begun a part of your journey that will likely take you places you can't foresee. That's true of all of us, though, to varying degrees.

I've always thought of the word "valiant" when I thought of you, Lou Anne, and never known why. Now that I understand more about you, I see valor. (Did you know that valor has its roots in a word that means worth, by the way?)

I replied.

It's interesting that you used the word "valor." Laura and Janie both say I have courage, but I feel so much the opposite. I'm terrified of the future and the fact that I haven't faced the tip of the iceberg in what will inevitably come to test my emotions, my resolve, and my ability to make the right decisions. It's as if I am teetering on the edge of a cliff, not knowing which way I will fall. At times I feel as if I'm taking it one day at a time, and other times I feel I'm existing an hour at a time. I keep telling myself my life will get better, but I know it will get much, much worse before things improve. I just keep telling myself to hold it together for a little longer.

Barbara and I kept up a running e-mail correspondence all day, and she encouraged me to be patient and try to become comfortable with myself. Finally she made a statement that I'll never forget.

About valor—people think John McCain is a hero because he endured less than five years' captivity and torture. You endured almost thirty-seven years, and, I believe, you're still working your way out of captivity.

Although her words validated my years of suffering, I felt a twinge of guilt having my thirty-seven years with Jim compared to actual physical torture. McCain had endured a much worse life during his five years than I had during my thirty-seven.

❧ ❧ ❧ ❧

Feeling a little better, I wrote J.W., my eldest son, and emphasized that he could tell anyone he wished that he has a gay mother, but asked him to let me know who he told so if someone gave me a funny look at church the next day, I'd know why.

Early Sunday morning, he updated me. He'd received nothing but positive reactions, and one of his friends had commented, "Your mother really has a lot of courage."

The Sunday-school lesson went well, the group much larger than usual. Many went out of their way to compliment me on the lesson I taught.

Janie walked with me to the parking lot, saying. "Your lessons are so good, Lou Anne. You really ought to tape them. You do save them, don't you?"

"Yes, but they aren't that original. I just gather material from lots of different sources and put it all together."

As we talked, Janie didn't pay attention to where she was going among the cars in the church parking lot and ran into a rearview mirror. She got quite a jolt and probably a bad bruise. I exclaimed, "Oh, honey! Are you hurt?"

She didn't seem to react abnormally to my words, but I knew I'd goofed and hoped she didn't give my endearment more thought later on.

I knew I had to get over my feelings for her, yet I couldn't imagine living my life without ever seeing or

talking to her. My fantasy world returned as I thought
how wonderful it would be to drive somewhere with
Janie beside me. It would be a dream come true.

❧ ❧ ❧ ❧

When I attended a supper before Sunday-evening
services a week later, two friends of both Jim and me
came by the table to greet me. They probably didn't
know that I knew that they knew about me. It was like
a game we were playing.

But I felt a different reaction from Josh's friend,
Charlie. He walked right by me, and I was sure he didn't
intend to speak to me. I looked him in the eye and
said, "Hi, Charlie," and he mumbled something as he
continued walking. Normally, he would have stopped
and asked, "What have you heard from Josh? How's he
doing?" But he didn't tonight. He seemed embarrassed
to have to look at me, which upset me.

Chapter Fourteen

During March, I wasn't sleeping much. When I called Janie one morning, we talked for over an hour. "I hope Jim finds someone special," she said, then added, "Lou Anne, you need someone in your life, someone to love. I hope you find such a person soon."

Thoughts of her raced through my mind as I mumbled, "Yes, that would be nice." She was right, of course. If someone else came into my life, that would help subdue my feelings toward her. I definitely needed to get over her. The divorce would be final in three weeks, and I looked forward to that time when I could truly feel free.

One afternoon I surfed the web and ended up on a web site that contained all kinds of horrible, despicable comments about homosexuals. Why are people so mean and cruel? How can any human being say such unkind, nasty things about another?

I was ready for an upward swing in my mood. I'd been down in the dumps longer than usual this time. I just wanted to crawl into bed and stay there and count the hours until I saw Janie the next day.

One morning I awoke extremely early and eventually got up around five thirty. I experienced an overwhelming feeling of sadness for the fourth straight day. Though I'd finally decided to free both Jim and me to find true happiness, my decision had introduced me to the most tremendous misery I'd ever faced. And to make matters worse, I'd fallen in love with a happily married woman. How could that happen?

Perhaps I needed to make a conscious move toward finding a partner, but I had absolutely no idea how to go about finding someone else. Sometimes I felt a desperate yearning to put my arms around a woman and just hold her.

❧❧❧❧

Laura, who had been visiting me during her spring break and was getting ready to leave, said to me, "Mother, I love you just the way you are. I wouldn't change one thing about you."

"Surely there are some things you'd prefer were different about me."

"No," she stated. "Not a thing. I'm real proud of you."

I found it practically unbelievable to understand why a daughter wouldn't prefer her mother to be straight rather than gay. Nevertheless her declaration uplifted my spirit.

❧❧❧❧

One Saturday afternoon in the middle of March, I attended a bridal shower at Janie's house for Carolyn's daughter. Carolyn, a former seminarian, is a very knowledgeable and supportive member of our Sunday-school class.

I was convinced some of the ladies attending the shower would know about me and might say something. By the time I left my apartment, a feeling of dread had overtaken me, and I began imagining condemning looks and/or comments. I was determined, however, to face whatever was thrown at me.

After arriving, I began to relax and actually enjoyed the gathering in Janie's beautiful home, filled with fine, expensive artwork. Once I caught sight of her as she stood close to a large mirror that reflected greenery and flowers. The sight almost took my breath away. I wanted to just stare but forced myself to look away. I didn't want her to see me looking at her. But I do believe that's the prettiest I've ever seen her. She was radiant.

When the shower ended, Carolyn's husband arrived in their car. Within my hearing, he informed one of the guests that Carolyn insists I'm the best Sunday-school teacher at First Baptist Church. Then he turned to me and began complimenting me on how nice I looked and how much he liked my dress. I was speechless. He'd always been nice to me, but he was extremely nice that afternoon, overly complimentary.

The Lord really does move in mysterious ways. I'd dreaded the occasion so much that I felt physically ill as I drove to Janie's, but when I left for home, wonderful compliments made my heart sing.

❧ ❧ ❧ ❧

At church Sunday evening, I again saw Charlie, Josh's friend. He'd been avoiding me and still won't look me in the eye. I again spoke directly to him, forcing him to reply. But it seemed almost more than he could handle, and he scooted away as quickly as he could. I felt challenged to make Charlie treat me as the friend he liked and respected. After all, I really was the same person.

৯৽৽৽৽৽

Several days later, Janie called to tell me about a conversation she had at one of the weddings she'd attended. Jim's friend, Milton, had made a point of walking over to her and saying, "Thank you for being such a good friend to Lou Anne. I know how difficult and painful it is for her at this time, and I appreciate your helping her out."

As Janie shared Milton's words, my mind seemed to shut down from amazement. Their conversation must have been an extended one, but I recall little of what else she related. I do recall Janie told Milton, "I'm sure this is also a difficult time for Jim." Milton agreed, yet returned to the subject of me and the "brave step" I'd taken. Milton was probably Jim's best friend. Since neither Milton, nor his wife, had spoken to me, his sympathy and understanding came as a welcome surprise.

It was hard for me to explain, even to myself, why the loving, kind reactions from Barbara, Janie, Laura, J.W., Milton, and our pastor Bob Watson amazed me. It might have been related to living with a feeling of guilt all my life. It was such a part of me that I didn't understand why everyone else wasn't following my example and heaping additional feelings of guilt and sin on me.

So many emotions were rushing around inside of me then, some colliding against each other and bouncing off to head in different directions. Making them stand still long enough to truly analyze my feelings was impossible. I only knew that I expected different reactions than what I was getting. It was as if I wished someone would haul off and beat me to a pulp and get it all over with. Maybe that's what I wanted to do to myself. The physical pain appealed to me, like a cleansing or like something I deserved.

The one truth I continued to hang onto was that God loves me. Beyond that, I got all mixed up inside. I read a very interesting verse in Romans one day.

But who are you, O man, to talk back to God. Shall what is formed say to him who formed it, "Why did you make me like this?"

This verse became an affirmation that God deliberately formed me as a gay person and that I had no right to question His decision. This verse helped me feel good about myself and what I am.

≈≈≈≈

Day after day my depression seemed to get worse, especially after I attended the funeral of an acquaintance. The funeral was a celebration of a life well lived, certainly not a sad affair. Nevertheless, a longing to die came over me. I wished I could just leave and escape this world.

After the service, I stood in line to speak to the widow and the adult daughters of the deceased man. Several members of my Sunday-school class stood next to me, and in the course of the conversation, one mentioned a nineteen-year-old girl who'd recently committed suicide. "I just don't understand why anyone would do that," the person said.

Then she mentioned another suicide, a twenty-nine-year-old. I immediately wondered if perhaps one or both were gay. That would certainly explain, at least to me, why they'd taken such a step. Then one of the ladies said, "They shouldn't be allowed that option in solving their problems."

I so wanted to tell them how much I understood what those girls were bound to have gone through—the terrible loneliness, despair, misery, and eventual descent into hopelessness, which finally made them take that final step. I suppose neither of those two women next to me had ever experienced such a depression. I yearned to tell them what it was like, how I'd lived with it for many years, and how at that very moment I wanted so much to die that I was terribly nauseous. How shocked they would be.

But I realized neither of these ladies could possibly understand what my life had been like. Then my mind jumped to the Sunday-school lesson I planned to teach the next day. I might go too far in stepping on the toes of the Religious Right, but maybe God wanted me to do just that.

I was trying to get up the nerve to share some thoughts about Christians that I'd gleaned from Philip Yancey's book, *What's So Amazing About Grace.* How would they react if I talked about how many people today associate evangelism with a message of hate and that the reputation Jesus earned as a lover of sinners was in danger of being lost today? Would they listen if I told them what a prostitute recently said when someone invited her to attend church? *Church! Why would I ever go there? I was already feeling terrible about myself. They'd just make me feel worse!* So-called Christians have come a long way from Christ's example to love one another, and I wanted to tell my class exactly that.

Chapter Fifteen

Toward the end of March, I talked with my pastor, Bob Watson, about my sexual orientation. At the beginning, I found it difficult to know what to say, but his kindness led me to share with him quite a bit about my life and what it had been like to pretend to be heterosexual. I wanted to ask him whether I should tell my Sunday-school class about my sexual orientation, and he advised me not to speak to them about it as a group, but to talk with one or two at a time. "If you talk to them as a group," he said, "you'll experience the very lowest opinions in that group."

Various church members were asking him if he was aware of my sexual orientation, he said, and assured me they weren't upset or condemning, but inquisitive. "I think you will be pleasantly surprised by all the support you will find among church members who think very highly of you," he told me.

"Can you tell me who's come to you that already knows about me?"

He looked rather uncomfortable. "No, I can't. And be prepared for others who will say some unkind things to you. Decide ahead of time what you will say to them." In fact, he urged me several times to be prepared.

"It might be a good idea for you to give up teaching your Sunday-school class, at least for a while," he also told me.

That statement took me by surprise. It shouldn't

have, but it did.

"How is your mother taking this news?" he asked.

"I haven't told her yet, and I'm not certain I will."

"You need to."

"I feel angry toward her. She knew when I was in college that I'd fallen in love with a girl, but she did nothing but condemn me. She also pressured me to get married—the same kind of pressure I felt from society. That's why I married Jim and lived a very unhappy life. I don't know if I'll ever discuss this with her."

"How is Jim taking this?"

"He seemed sad at first, but I think he's becoming angry now. That doesn't surprise me."

"Telling him the truth about yourself was an act of grace. You did a wonderful thing. How are your children taking the news?"

"Laura and J.W. are all right with it. Josh is having trouble, and I haven't heard from Michael. I know it's not easy for him. He's like his dad, and they're both very prejudiced against gays."

"You need to give them time."

"Yes, I know. I'm trying to. I'm certain the Graysons and the Herringtons know about me, but no one has said a word to me personally."

"You have to give people a chance. This is all new to them. You're probably the only homosexual they've ever known. They don't know what to say. Just don't begin a crusade. Whatever you do, share this information on a one-on-one basis. Are you taking care of yourself? Exercising? You've lost a lot of weight, haven't you?"

"Yes, but I'm watching it. I do exercise, and I walk a little."

I sighed. "I keep asking myself why I've had to

suffer so much, and I'm beginning to believe that God wants me to do something. That's why I've had to come out of hiding. You can't imagine how wonderful it would have been to have had someone to talk with when I was a teenager and was confused about my feelings. There are bound to be other people in this church just like me—each hiding in his or her little cubbyhole of fear and secrecy. I want to do something for them, especially the children who'll grow up feeling the same guilt and condemnation I always did."

"There probably is a reason all of this has happened to you," he said. "Just be patient, and those needing help will eventually find you."

≈≈≈≈≈

After our conversation, I walked upstairs to the Wednesday-night supper, picked up my tray of food, and sat among friends. Nancy Grayson took time to come over and speak to me, even touching me on the shoulder. I was overjoyed to have someone touch me. It was as if she was saying that I'm still human, not some monster she didn't want to have any contact with.

Late this evening, I wrote to Barbara, sharing with her my conversation with Bob. Her reply was encouraging and included the following paragraph.

As I told my Sunday-school class recently, my all-time favorite poster shows a pool of light (as if from a flashlight) surrounded by darkness and the words, "Faith is going to the edge of all the light you have, and taking one more step." I suspect that may be where you are. But if you're walking in the Light, you'll be able to see when you take that step.

I hoped she was right because I certainly felt as if I was walking in darkness, not knowing what would happen next and how others would react to me. The possibility that, as I took each step on my journey of coming out, I would have light at that last minute to guide me was a comforting assurance.

❧.❧.❧.❧

Surprise! Only two days later I seemed to be doing much, much better. My fantasies weren't so much a part of my life any more. What a relief! And, generally speaking, I was sleeping a little better and had gained a pound. I had to admit, though, that maybe I had such a good day yesterday because Janie called me twice— early in the morning and again close to suppertime. We chatted for over an hour each time. Just friendly talk. I finally felt that I was being as good a friend to her in these conversations as she had been to me.

My pastor e-mailed me an even longer explanation of why he thought I should reveal myself to members of our church one at a time and resign from teaching Sunday school. After I read it, I began to tremble with both hope and despair. I was glad he didn't condemn me but upset that he'd asked me to quit teaching my class of adult women.

I immediately forwarded his letter to both Barbara and Janie, then went for a long, fast-paced walk. As I strode along, I prayed for strength and thanked God for giving me some really good days recently.

Barbara immediately replied, agreeing with our pastor's advice and encouraging me to continue to bear my burdens. She said she was grateful I'd allowed her to accompany me on my journey so far and that she'd already learned so much from me. But she also encouraged me to go slowly.

Sometimes it's extremely irritating to those of us who are quick, to have to move at the pace of the slower members of our flock, but that's pretty well the speed at which flocks move, isn't it?

I could understand the reasons Barbara and my pastor advised me to move slowly. People needed time to adjust to something with which they had so little experience and had ignored for so long.

But my twenty-one-year-old daughter, Laura, didn't understand the church members' attitudes and prejudices and the potential problems my coming out could cause within the church. This is the daughter who months prior to my coming out had said to me one day, "Mom, I have lots of gay friends and I'm convinced they can't help being gay."

I had been thrilled to hear her words and tempted at that time to tell her she had a gay mother. But I hadn't. However, when I knew I needed to share my secret with someone, I chose to talk to her. With her accepting attitude toward gays, she was "safe." Laura represents the younger generation, which has a more open and accepting attitude.

I felt torn between generational experiences and attitudes.

Chapter Sixteen

After much thought, I decided to follow my pastor's advice and sent a long e-mail to Carolyn, one of the best-educated members of my Sunday-school class. In it, I explained how long I'd wanted a divorce, shared Jim's letter to me and my reply, and then told her that our pastor thought I should no longer teach our class. I even sent her a copy of Dr. Watson's recent long letter.

Carolyn replied the next morning.

Lou Anne, you probably thought that I would be knocked out of my chair when I read your e-mail, but I wasn't. Janie and I have discussed this issue in the past. I, like Dr. Watson, think there is too much homophobia and hurt associated with it. I certainly will be discreet with the information. If I were you, I would not make a public statement in the class and would be very careful about who I shared it with. I would hate to see you hurt further by all of this. And I hate the thought of losing you for a teacher. You are such a wonderful leader, but you need to follow God's direction in that one. You have so much to share with others, and I know how much I gain from all of our classes.

I must admit that I am still very convoluted in my feelings about homosexuality. I have really wrestled with the Baptist Old Testament doctrine about Sodom and Gomorrah and the wickedness there. I also know that

Jesus was the last person to condemn anyone and was most loving and understanding. I am so sorry that you have had so many feelings of depression and wishes for death. I KNOW that is not what God wants. I certainly do not think homosexuality is a sin. People can be involved in unhealthy relationships whether heterosexual or homosexual. I still struggle with the idea of same-sex relationships. I don't have any idea if you just didn't want to live a lie anymore or would like to have a life partner. That is totally between you and God. I couldn't and wouldn't pretend to give an opinion on that one.

Lou Anne, be assured that this does not affect my respect for you or our friendship in any way. I don't know many people who would have had the courage to face the situation head-on like you have. I admire you for that. I grieve at the pain you have suffered and just wish there was some way I could help make it better. Thank you for trusting me enough as a friend to share this information with me. Like I said earlier, I honor your privacy in this matter. I would be glad to talk with you any time you need to.

Carolyn

I thanked her and told her that I was learning other ways to look at the Old Testament verses she referred to, then shared new interpretations with her.

Then I wrote Barbara that I was leaning pretty heavily toward resigning, and she encouraged me to use the word sabbatical rather than resignation.

Prior to teaching the Sunday-school lesson that week, I privately handed our class president, Patsy, a sealed envelope containing copies of Jim's and my letters that outed me and told her to wait until she got home to read what was inside. I so hoped she wouldn't open the envelope then but would wait as I'd instructed. I wasn't at all certain I could properly handle her reaction in that public setting, and I wasn't at all certain what kind of reaction she might have.

❦❦❦❦

Patsy called that afternoon, shocked. She kept saying that all of us have sin in our lives, but as she kept reassuring me that we all have sin, I kept asking myself what made being a homosexual a sin? She had no concept of whether I'd ever acted upon those desires, yet she still considered me a sinner simply because I was gay. I don't know how many times she made that statement, but I never threw it back at her in any way. I was just thankful she was so loving and understanding.

My conversation with Patsy drained me, yet I was delighted she'd taken the time to call. Afterward, although I was terribly depressed and teary-eyed, I decided to eat supper at the church. The simple meal was delicious, but I continued to get teary-eyed off and on during the service and talked with Barbara afterward. She reached over and steadied my hand, which was shaking as I held my glass of iced tea.

❦❦❦❦

Jim called that evening to discuss details of our financial arrangement. During our conversation I shared with him that I would soon be resigning from teaching my class and mentioned that members of the church were starting to contact Dr. Watson about me.

Jim said, "Well, surely they aren't coming in support of you!"

I found that comment strange. Did he want to assure himself that others were condemning me? "Watson says they're contacting him out of concern for me. Hold on just a minute and I'll read his letter to you," which I did.

He had nothing to say afterward.

ᘓᘓᘓᘓᘓ

Having decided to resign from teaching, I began working on my last Sunday-school lesson to my class. I also spent time just sitting and reading some of the Psalms—and crying, keeping the tissue box beside my chair.

Barbara had written to me earlier, saying that my sabbatical could be a healing time for me and others. But an icy coldness swept over me. I put my arms through a sweater and wrapped my legs in a throw blanket, then looked out my window onto a cold, dreary day. Unrelenting pain had lodged itself in my heart.

Chapter Seventeen

G ood news today. The mail had finally brought me a letter from Michael! I anxiously opened the envelope.

> *Dear Mother,*
> *I am writing you this note not because I can't or don't want to visit with you personally, but because I need the forum of being able to make my point without the distraction of a give-and-take discussion.*
> *I love you because you're the reason I'm on this earth, and because I'm reasonably happy with the way I've turned out*
> *If you told me you needed me to stand on my head and sing nursery rhymes in a prison visiting room, I'd do it for you. Put simply, any decision or action you take in regard to your coming out is okay with me. I support you. Your happiness is more important to me than my own.*
> *You are who you are based on what you have said and how you have acted over the course of your life. You are defined by the actions of your children, whose greatest role model is the person reading this note. I agree that sexuality is a major part of the human experience, but that it is a paltry standard by which to evaluate others.*
> *Frankly, I don't understand the positive benefits of sharing this with others. If it is what you want, I support you. If it is not what you want, then I need to have a talk with Dad, because he is under the opposite impression.*

I love Dad, too, but he may not be totally objective when it comes to sharing his wife's secret. After all, you've just provided him an opportunity to completely abdicate any role he may have played in his failed marriage.

In closing, I hope the next time you feel depressed you will think about me and how much I love you.

Michael

What a wonderful letter, from a wonderful son.

However, I then received an e-mail from Gwen Patterson of the Christian Women's Job Corps. Her four-page, single-spaced letter ended with these paragraphs.

I miss you. I love you in the Lord as a sister. I know that you are going through much pain and suffering, and probably have more to come. I hurt for you and cry for your choice. But I still do not reject you, only the choice you are making.

I am praying that the Lord will hedge you in and grant you repentance that will lead to a knowledge of the truth, and that you will come to your senses and escape from the trap of the devil, who has taken you captive to do his will (2 Timothy 2:25b-26).

Seek counsel with those who have won the victory over the temptations of homosexuality. When you are ready, help will be available from caring brothers and sisters in Christ.

Yours in Christ Jesus,
Gwen Patterson

I kept seeing the words "escape from the trap of the devil." That's exactly what I did when I became honest with myself about who and what I am. The devil no longer had a hold on me, infusing me with fear, shame, and guilt. I told myself that I was finally free to be the person God created me to be. Free to live my life in the way He ordains. Free, wonderfully free! Delightfully free.

When I awoke very early the next morning, I decided to just go ahead and get up. I immediately sat down and wrote Barbara, updating her. I expressed my concern about becoming emotional when I taught my last lesson on Sunday and ended by saying that I'd love to be able to give that lesson without being so tense and on edge. "Know of anyone who'd give me a tranquilizer to use that morning? I'm serious."

I then told her that the court hearing for the divorce was scheduled for 8:15 Tuesday morning, April 11. "Just one more step along this road I'm on."

A while later, Janie called. Hallelujah! We talked for over an hour and a half. As always, she was very supportive and quite upset that I was leaving the class. She said her husband just couldn't believe I'd been asked to quit. I was so down yesterday because she hadn't called me, but then she called and I was floating on air.

Barbara wrote me a long, insightful e-mail mid-morning. It was full of news and support. She encouraged me to see my doctor and ask him to prescribe a mild sedative.

〽〽〽〽

I decided to take Barbara's advice and drove to my doctor's office to be worked into his schedule. This meant a two-hour wait. As I sat there, I re-read a letter I'd just received from my brother Tom, to whom I'd recently come out.

Your letter made me smile. I didn't even have to be sitting down to read it, because the only part of it that was a big surprise was that you were speaking up and speaking out. Congratulations.

Mom has never talked to me in any depth about you. Back when you roomed with Karen, she said a couple of things that indicated she was worried, and I know she wanted you and Karen to separate. I acted like it was no big deal even though I secretly thought the two of you were in love. Whatever she thought, she kept between her and Dad.

I don't have any advice about talking to Mom. Our family (and South Texas culture) was so hung up about sex that even though Mom has become more tolerant, she still has a way to go, as far as accepting people without prejudice. Don't let the bottomless pits pull on you. It must be quite a shock to do what you are doing. I don't think I would ever have that kind of nerve.

Your confidences are safe with me. I wish you the best.

As always, Tom

I smiled, then tried to read the mystery novel I'd taken with me, but I couldn't concentrate, which was very unusual. Thoughts of Janie kept coming to my mind—the kind of thoughts I shouldn't have.

When Dr. Morris finally entered the examination room, I quickly told him exactly what I'd been going through recently. By then, I was fighting the urge to break down and bawl. "I just need something to get me through this next Sunday, when I'll be teaching my last Sunday-school lesson," I managed to say.

Dr. Morris told me about several available medications but decided Xanax would be best for me because it takes effect quicker than the others.

Then he sat down and began telling me about his numerous brothers and sisters and that being gay wasn't completely new to his family. "I have a younger sister," he explained, "who adopted two girls, and one of these girls decided to be gay."

When he said "decided to be gay," my hackles began to rise. No fool would decide to be gay! But I kept quiet and listened. However, what he said next made me even angrier. "She's still welcomed into the family. She was even invited to one of the family weddings."

Even invited! The nerve! Why wouldn't she be invited? But I didn't voice these thoughts either. Over and over he talked about how this girl had *decided* to be gay.

Finally, I couldn't take it any longer. "This is not a decision!"

He agreed it probably wasn't, that it was a bad choice of words. He said the latest research indicated that homosexuality is connected to hormones.

Then as he walked out of the room to write up the prescription, he turned to me and asked, "What church do you attend?"

"First Baptist," I replied. "Thank goodness I don't go to Green Acres Baptist!" (Green Acres is the largest Baptist church in Tyler and is very fundamentalist/ conservative.)

He then started laughing, really laughing, and assured me, "I'm not laughing at you. I'm laughing with you."

The nurse phoned in the prescription, and I left and headed straight for the pharmacy. I needed that Xanax.

꘏꘏꘏꘏

That night I took my first Xanax, and when I awoke the next morning a little after three a.m., I took another pill. It worked. I slept until 7:15! Unbelievable.

Tom, my brother, had written me a long e-mail, saying he agreed that I shouldn't talk with Mom unless it became necessary some day. He then encouraged me to learn how to have fun, not try to do too much too fast, and to be easy on myself. He also advised me to go explore the feelings of affection I've kept bottled up for so long.

Talk to other women who AGREE with you rather than with those who disagree with you. Find a gay and lesbian support group in Tyler or Longview or Dallas, and attend their meetings for a while. Skip church, and go elsewhere some weeks. Concentrate on developing one or two close personal friendships. It doesn't mean you'll have sex, but it does mean you'll be putting your time and energy into exploring yourself rather than into combating or converting others.

If you were shooting rapids down a canyon river (which, incidentally, you are!), and you could see a huge standing hydraulic turbulence, wouldn't you steer around it, rather than into it? And can't you apply that same wisdom socially? The very thought takes me back to hippie days when the question was: Would you rather fight or make love? Which is better for you personally? Which sets a better example for humankind?

It's not your job to lead others, and it's not their job to help you. It's your job to save yourself. The first step in that direction is to get help. Find women who have already been where you are, and let them guide you. Tell them your story, and then listen to theirs.

Tom then provided numerous web sites and phone numbers for organizations such as PFLAG, SPROUTS, TWIGS, GLAAD, along with Dallas's suicide and crisis center and another Dallas group that promotes the validity of same-sex couples. (PFLAG stands for Parents, Families and Friends of Lesbians and Gays. SPROUTS is a group of women who are questioning their sexuality. TWIGS is a group of women in gay society. GLAAD is the Gay and Lesbian Alliance Against Defamation.)

Okay. I've spoken my piece. My hunch is that as soon as you find another woman or two with whom you can openly share, the suicide thoughts and terrible sadness will evaporate, and you will have a chance at the happiness that eluded you while you were trying to live a life molded for you by others.

My love and best wishes go with you, sister.
Tom

I forwarded his words to Barbara, then cried and cried for hours without stopping. Not only did I experience Tom's love and concern, but his wisdom overwhelmed me. He knew exactly what he was talking about.

≈≈≈≈

Barbara agreed with Tom's advice and encouraged me to follow it and to search for online resources as well. She mentioned www.truluck.com, which contained Rembert Truluck's story and a ton of Bible commentary. He was a former Baptist preacher who went to Baptist seminaries, taught in a Baptist college, etc.

And after several days of sadness and depression, during which I agonized about my reply to Tom, I finally wrote him.

Just to know that you perceived the love that Karen and I felt for each other overwhelmed me.

You're right. I never learned how to have fun. Karen and I had fun. But behind that fun was the ever-present awareness that society and parents prohibited our relationship from being permanent. We savored every moment we had together as if it were our last—and sure enough, that day came sooner than we anticipated.

After we separated, fun, joy, friendship, and love went out of my life, and, as you so aptly put it, I began to live a life molded for me by others. I became a shell of a person, a person I eventually came to hate. I spent my life distancing myself from ever forming a close friendship with a female for fear of what might happen to me. And I know now that was a most wise decision on my part because I have fallen hopelessly, desperately in love with my friend, Janie, who is heterosexual and has no idea what I feel toward her. It's killing me and I have to get over this. I am in the depths of an emotional turmoil that I have never before faced.

I have contacted a local chapter of PFLAG and have been given their meeting date, time, and location. I plan to go. It's going to be tough, but I've never had an opportunity to talk with someone who has endured the kind of life I have endured. I need to do this.

I appreciate the references you sent. I've spent my whole life in denial, never even reading about homosexuality. Even now I've read only two books on the subject. I believed if I ignored the subject, it would

go away. Now I know differently.
   Dear, dear brother, thank you so much.
   Lou Anne

Mid-afternoon, a letter arrived from my daughter, Laura.

I think about you all the time and hope you're doing all right. Just remember that lots of people love and care about you (me being #1). You're doing the right thing—which isn't always easy.
   I love you and can't wait till you come to Lubbock before graduation and we can pack up my belongings together!
   Laura

Her letter brought a smile, along with a feeling of warm hugs. I looked forward to helping her move from Lubbock to Austin at the end of May.

Chapter Eighteen

After spending the afternoon at Mother's, I arrived at church in time for the Wednesday-evening meal prior to the service. I sat at a table with Barbara and her husband and two other couples. When I got up to refill my iced tea, Carl Atkins, one of the men seated there who's about my age, asked me, "How are you liking retirement?"

I actually laughed at him and said, "That's the funniest question I've heard in a long time," then walked away to fill my glass.

I realized later that Barbara had tried to cover up for my rudeness by saying, "Lou Anne's going through some really tough times right now."

"She made her bed, and now she has to lie in it," he'd said.

During this exchange, the others at our table had already left to work with various children's choirs. Barbara, Jack (her husband), and Carl were the only ones left at the table. Barbara told me later that Carl's comment upset her husband so much that he outed me to Carl.

Barbara said that Carl actually seemed to take it quite well and seemed sympathetic. But Barbara was upset with her husband for blabbing and told Carl to keep this information confidential—that Jack shouldn't have said anything.

Carl had retorted, "I have to tell my wife, of

course."

Barbara must have really climbed all over her husband for talking about me, but strangely, it didn't bother me that the truth was being told.

I told her not to worry about it and to assure her husband that I wasn't upset with him. After all, I figured it'd eventually all come out anyway. What was wrong with one more person knowing about it?

⁂

When I returned from church, a letter from my brother, Tom, awaited me in which he urged me to get a substitute to teach my Sunday-school class.

> *You don't owe anyone any explanation. And you don't need anyone else's approval for being who you are. But to do this, you have to be beyond the crying state, and you've written that you're still there. Don't fight it. Let it last as long as it wants to, for it's a process that releases old blocked emotions. You'll eventually reach the point where your tears turn to smiles and laughter.*
>
> *Then again, maybe the Xanax will kick the weepiness out of you immediately, and you can handle everything with equilibrium. Personally, I'd opt out of Sunday school ahead of time, let someone else take over, go for a walk in the woods on Sunday morning (if it's not stormy), and let events take their own course.*
>
> *Now I've got to quit offering advice. Once again, I congratulate you for being willing to be in touch with all of yourself. At times I used to wonder what happened to that tough little sister I used to play with—the one who rode pretend wild horses and shot pretend cowboy villains and who often demonstrated that her biceps were*

bigger than mine. Now I have every confidence that she's survived and will be part of your life again.

More power to you...Tom

❧ ❧ ❧ ❧

Later, Janie called and we talked a full two hours, until after midnight. How refreshing. We discussed her plans to travel to Austin the next day, her experience of falling in love almost instantaneously with her husband, Charles, and her yearnings for time to call her own. After finally hanging up, I called Laura, who was still awake.

"What in the world were you doing on the phone all this time?" she asked.

"Talking with Janie."

"You sound so much better tonight, Mother. I bet it has to do with your conversation with Janie."

"Yes, I'm sure that's the reason. I so enjoy talking with her."

After hanging up, I wrote to Barbara to tell her that Jim calls Laura often to tell her everything. She said that Gwen Patterson from the Christian Women's Job Corps had called him recently and kept him on the phone for over an hour.

Gwen talked about me and how wrong I was in my choice and how she was praying for me. She felt I'd come to my senses and return to him because the Bible is quite clear that I'm doing wrong. Jim finally got fed up and told her that if she believed everything that was in the Bible, then she'd know that women are never to speak up in church! I can't help but be proud of him for that answer.

Then I told Barbara that Jim and I were starting to have some disagreements about some of the financial arrangements, but I thought we could work through them in an amicable way. At least I hoped so.

The next morning I read a note from Carolyn, written at one a.m., saying that even though she would be in Waco Saturday, she planned to be in Sunday school this week, as this would be my last day as their teacher. I learned after the fact that she had to make an extremely late drive in order to be present. I was deeply touched, as her actions demonstrated her support and the importance of our friendship.

❧❧❧❧

Sunday, I awoke earlier than I had been, despite taking a Xanax. I had ample time to shower, wash my hair, dress, eat, and review my Sunday-school lesson. I went over and over it aloud until I felt capable of getting through it with ease. However, I was definitely on edge and teary. I knew I was in trouble and kept reminding myself to just read the lesson without trying to ad lib. That would be much safer.

So I practiced reading without thinking, but it didn't work. The tears still came. I was determined, however, to deliver this last lesson. I'd worked hard on it, felt it was well prepared, and I wanted to teach it.

I attended the eight thirty a.m. worship service and even then occasionally fought back tears. The Sunday-school lesson was from Luke 13:10-17 and was titled "What's More Important—Rules or People?" Although this was an assigned topic, it was a very fitting lesson for my situation. I explained to the class that Jesus was a great teacher because He forced people to think, which angered others, especially the ruler of the synagogue.

As I spoke, I did just fine with the exposition of the Biblical passage. I then switched gears.

"I began this lesson talking about Jesus being a great teacher, and one of the attributes of a great teacher is the ability to enable the student to find inner direction. A great teacher helps you find your own goal. Those around you no longer determine your goals. You begin to march to a different drummer. You find a whole new direction from God. Many of us are guilty of radar living. Our radar is always out, picking up moods. We're other-directed. We try to fit in, make it, be right with the crowd."

I don't recall where I gleaned some of these thoughts, but most of my lessons pulled in writings from many different sources. The only original portion of my lessons was the way I spliced together all I gathered.

I continued. "Jesus refused to be other-directed. When He is warned that King Herod is out to get Him, He replies that this sly fox is not going to set His agenda. He is going to continue to minister for the next three days and beyond, with no change of plan.

"It seems to me there are two ways that those who are other-directed can be trapped. They can try to please others or be stubbornly determined to rebel against any and all suggestions or directions. To be inner-directed means that our inner voice dictates our agenda, that 'still, small voice' of which the Bible speaks in I Kings 19:12.

"Robert Louis Stevenson wrote, 'To know what you prefer instead of humbly saying *Amen* to what the world tells you that you ought to prefer is to have kept your soul alive.' That's what Jesus demonstrates for us toward the end of this chapter. We have kept our soul alive when we are inner-directed through the voice of the Holy Spirit."

Somewhere in this part of the lesson I began to lose control. My voice began to break, and tears sprang to my eyes. I finally just had to stop. At that point I explained to the class, "I really thought I could do this, but I'm not certain I can."

Someone in the class said, "Just give it a few minutes." I did, but time wasn't helping me gain control. Janie then said, "I'm going to pull my chair over next to Lou Anne. Carolyn, you pull your chair up on the other side, and the rest of you move close. Let's surround Lou Anne and let her know how much we care for her."

And that's what everyone did as they waited silently until I was able to continue speaking. Even so, as I kept reading, I periodically had to stop to gain control of myself. I said, "I'm not going to sit here in front of you and say that the Holy Spirit is directing me to make a change in my life, but I'm also not going to say that isn't true. Time will tell. But I can honestly say that I am taking a route with my life in tune with what Robert Louis Stevenson wrote. In other words, I'm keeping my soul alive by knowing what I prefer in opposition to what the world tells me I ought to prefer.

"I'm making some changes in my life and these changes remind me of a story I recently read in Dr. James C. Denison's daily devotions that illustrates in a very vivid way what seems to be happening to me. Let's say that the life I thought I was going to lead is similar to that of planning to take a journey, a journey to—let me just say France, because the actual destination is insignificant. I've prepared all my life to go to France. I've packed the right things. I've learned to speak French. I've even learned to cook French food. I've studied French art. I know all about the country. And I can't wait to get there. I plan to take France by storm. I'm ready. And I get on the plane and start for France.

"But right before I land, the pilot says, 'Welcome to Germany.' And I say, 'Oh, my.' And I panic and run up the aisle and I say to the pilot, 'You've made a mistake. I'm not going to Germany. I'm going to France. I'm all ready. I'm packed. It's going to be perfect. Everyone's waiting for me there.'

"The pilot smiles and says, 'But we're going to Germany. Let's see what you think.' And I reluctantly return to my seat. I get my bags, lots of bags that were packed perfectly because I've planned for this all of my life. I have just the right things, and I'll look great.

"And the pilot says, 'You don't need all those bags. I have other bags for you. I've already packed them. I've prepared them. They're much lighter than those. And they're filled with gifts.' So you say, 'Oh, you have presents for me.' And he says, 'These are presents we're going to give away. They are gifts of acceptance and joy and love. The baggage will be very light.'

"I deplane to find a tandem bike waiting for me. And the pilot says, 'You take the front seat, and I'll just hop on the back.' I get on the front seat and start to pedal in circles. All the maps for France are in the bags. I knew all about France, but I don't know anything about Germany. I can't do this. So the pilot smiles and says, 'Would you like to trade places? I'll lead us.'

"So I get on the backseat and he begins to show me Germany. It's beautiful. And I begin to learn the German language and meet the German people. I see Bavaria. I realize that I never knew all of this was here. It's wonderful. I start to give the gifts away, and I start to receive many gifts in return. I even teach English to some of the German children there. And quite often I run into people who are busily coming and going from France. They say, 'It's a wonderful place.' And I say, 'Yes, I know. I was supposed to go there. I had it planned all along. But my pilot had a different journey for me and my pilot took me to a different place. It's beautiful, too.'"

The tears came again, and in a few minutes, I finished the lesson by saying, "You see, I'd planned to teach you ladies for years. I really enjoy this class and look forward to each and every Sunday. I thought this was what I was supposed to do. But I know now that it isn't, and I'm being led in a totally different direction. I'm hoping that some time in the future I can 'leave Germany and come back to France,' but I don't know if that will ever be possible. So I'll be stepping down as your teacher after today. You'll have a substitute next week, and I've pleaded with our associate pastor, Wilson Rhodes, to find you a permanent teacher very soon. I'll keep reminding him of this need, but you need to keep reminding him also.

"I read a sermon this past week delivered by a Canadian pastor that may help explain some of the changes taking place in my life. He described two ways I can talk to you. I can speak to you as a group, laying out concepts drawn from scripture, and hope and pray that you latch onto them and apply them in your own situations. But I could speak to you individually so that I wouldn't need to talk in generalities, as I would to a group. Speaking one-on-one is much more risky than speaking in great sweeping statements. It involves relationships and trust and honesty. You can't hide in face-to-face, soul-to-soul communication.

"I think Jesus knew this all too well. In today's

gospel story, Jesus was in the synagogue teaching a bunch of people. Then suddenly there appears a woman, and Jesus stops teaching and calls this woman over to him. A group message just became personal. That's the way Jesus works best: one-on-one, face-to-face, soul to soul. Only then does He have our full attention. And I think the lessons I will be sharing in the future will be one-on-one lessons instead of group lessons. That seems to be where I am being led."

We ended the class in our usual way, by all standing in a circle, joining hands, bowing our heads, and reciting together, "May the Lord watch between me and thee while we are absent one from the other." Afterward, each member hugged me and told me how much she loved and appreciated me. Finally, the only ones left in the room with me were Janie and Carolyn. Then Carolyn's husband walked in and joined us. All three gave me a pep talk, and Carolyn's husband said, "You shouldn't resign, Lou Anne. You really shouldn't."

"I must. You know I must," I replied.

"No," he said. "I don't think you should. I don't think you should at all." Janie then joined him by saying, "My husband said he doesn't think she should resign either. He thinks it's just awful she's been asked to quit."

Although their affirmations were kind and encouraging, my nerves were taut. I knew I needed to resign, and this was one of those occasions when the longer it's drawn out, the more difficult it becomes. Carolyn and her husband asked me to join them for lunch at a Chinese buffet. I dearly love Chinese food but had no appetite. I didn't want them to waste money on a buffet meal I couldn't eat so declined their kind offer. When I did, Carolyn promised to come by that afternoon to visit with me.

Later in the day, after returning from a walk, my heart leapt when I heard Janie's voice on my answering machine.

Hello, Lou Anne. It's Janie. I'm just calling to say hello and that I love you and that I've had two calls from Sunday-school class members today. One, I think, had no clue as to why you resigned from the position of teaching, and one I think knew exactly. The one who knew exactly said, 'We're going to Germany together.' So anyway, I wanted you to know that everybody loves you and is very distressed that you've left. You wouldn't believe all the positive things class members have said about you. You need to know this. These wonderful and understanding ladies love you. I just wanted to pass that message on to you. I love you, girl. Bye.

Carolyn came over later to visit, and we had a long, open talk. Afterward, we went to Paco's for Mexican food, and I amazed her with how much I ate. I do enjoy Mexican food. I also enjoyed being with Carolyn.

The following day she left a message for me on my answering machine.

I think it is evident that the word is out and you are officially out of the closet—be that wanted or not. For the most part, the response has been very caring. I didn't feel that most people were shocked, but truly concerned and had lots of questions. I've tried to be very positive. I haven't brought the subject up with anyone, but they all say, "You do know what's going on, don't you?' I let them tell me. They question whether you left Jim for another person, and I assure them that's not so—that you had to find release from an unbearable situation and live a life you felt was honest. Maybe things won't be as bad as feared. I am sure you've had calls and questions also. My prayers are with you in the morning as you go to court to finalize your divorce. I hope all goes well. If there's anything that I can do, please let me know.

You know my thoughts continue to be with you. You're a very special friend, and I'm proud to say so. Relax, eat, take a few deep breaths, and I'll talk to you soon!

    Carolyn

❧.❧.❧.❧

I got quite courageous Monday night. After handbell practice I attended for the first time a PFLAG meeting. I think I counted twenty-seven in attendance, some really nice people. Much of the discussion dealt with Christian beliefs and the treatment gays have received from their churches. It was a good place for me to be that night.

Driving to the church where PFLAG met took courage, but not nearly as much courage as it took for me to get out of the car and walk into the meeting. This was my first experience in outing myself to total strangers. I had no idea what to expect. I just knew it was important to meet other people like me, people I hoped would understand my embarrassing, shameful secret. The friends and family with whom I'd shared my story had been kind and loving, but had absolutely no clue as to what my life had been like. I felt a need to meet others like me.

I was feeling anxious as I walked in. Part of me wanted to turn and run, part of me recognized what a wonderful opportunity this experience could be for

me, and part of me was curious as to what gays and
lesbians looked like and acted like because I was just
as much a victim of misinformation as everyone else.
I walked in and sat down by a woman who seemed to
be alone. She was younger than I, attractive, about my
height and weight, with brown hair in a short haircut
like mine. Since no one was sitting with her and there
were few empty seats, she seemed the logical person for
me to sit beside.

The group was almost evenly divided between
men and women—men sitting with men, women with
women, all ages. I later learned they represent a cross-
section of our city as far as occupations, talent, and
economic status. Partners were sitting comfortably
beside each other. A few were openly affectionate. Those
who belonged together were relaxed and at ease in
letting others know they were partners.

I'd seen this only once before—when I attended
a Metropolitan Community Church in Lubbock about
three months earlier. At that time, my breath was
literally taken away when I walked into the church and
saw same-sex couples sitting together either holding
hands or one draping an arm around the other. I'd sat
toward the back of that sanctuary and cried during
the whole service. They were beautiful. I envied their
happiness, their sense of ease and relaxation, their
freedom to worship together as partners, their taking
communion together with their arms around each other.
The whole scenario was more than I could contain. Oh,
how I longed to have someone with whom to share my
life.

A fellowship had been held following that service
in Lubbock. I stayed to meet some of the congregation
and was wonderfully ministered to and cared for by

these warm, loving people. Now, I was seeing much the same type of individuals and experiencing the same type of atmosphere in this PFLAG meeting, which seemed very similar to a church service.

The speakers confirmed that God truly does love us. Afterward, we divided into small groups, during which time we were invited to tell our own stories. I told mine—mentioning that my divorce was to be finalized in the morning. When I said that I'd been married for thirty-seven years, they were amazed I'd stayed married that long. I was definitely an oddity in their eyes. Most of them had been married at one time or another and had children from those marriages, but their relationships had ended much, much sooner.

The woman I sat next to, Brenda, had been married for twenty years and had two grown sons.

The stories some of them told were heartbreaking—especially those of having their children taken away from them simply because they were gay. This was one thing I'd feared all of my life, especially on the few occasions when Jim was very angry and threatened me by saying, "I'm going to declare you an unfit mother and take the children away from you." I felt thankful my children were now grown.

By the time the meeting ended, I'd relaxed, made new friends, and looked forward to the next meeting.

Chapter Nineteen

Tuesday. The divorce was to be finalized that day. I was sure that's why I awakened so early. I updated Barbara about those in my class who knew about me and also told her about attending the PFLAG meeting. On that subject, I explained, "A great group of people—lots of talk about religion and God. They all feel ostracized from their churches."

When I arrived at the courthouse that morning, our lawyer was just walking in, so I joined him. Jim was already there. Since we'd been able to work everything out, we'd used the same lawyer and split the cost. We signed the necessary papers, and the appearance before the judge was rather cut and dried. He asked my name, had I lived in Smith County a set amount of time, the same question about the state of Texas, did I feel our differences could not be worked out, did we have any children under the age of eighteen, any expected, had we agreed on the financial division of property, etc. The judge asked Jim only three or four questions and gave him an opportunity to say whatever he wanted to or to contest anything. He chose not to speak, so the divorce was finalized in just a few minutes. Barbara had offered to come with me, but afterward I was glad I'd turned her down. Everything went very smoothly and quickly.

After we left the courthouse, I recalled that Jim had said he'd parked in our church's parking lot—about three blocks from the courthouse. I asked, "Would you like a ride to your car?"

He readily accepted, and I drove him there. He took my hand and said, "I wish it had never come to this."

"I wish it hadn't either."

"I still love you, but I hope both of us can find someone else to be happy with."

"I hope so, too. I really appreciate how nice you've been. You could have made it rough on me."

"I never wanted to do that." He began to cry and quickly exited my car. I drove away with a heavy heart, regretting that I'd hurt him like that.

⁂

The day after my divorce was final, I awoke feeling terribly sad.

An old friend who'd recently outed himself to me wrote to tell about a gay-oriented church in our community. St. Gabriel's, located south of Tyler and with a congregation of about a hundred warm, friendly members, had an Episcopalian-type service. The pastor was a gay woman and the majority of the congregation female.

He warned that I might not feel at home since I was a Baptist, but he said I could meet some like-minded people there and would probably enjoy discussing the pastor's interpretation of the Leviticus issues.

If you want to attend the church, I'll make an attempt to leave my church (St. Mattress—grin) and go with you. It's been several years since I've been there so most won't know me.

I replied immediately.

When I read your final sentence, I laughed out loud. Thanks. I really needed a laugh today. I appreciate the information but intend to stick with my church. These are the people who know me, and I plan to embrace this opportunity to be an example of a gay Christian.

And I did look at it as an opportunity for both the church and for me. Members of the church would have a chance to better understand and hopefully accept homosexuality, and I could be the good example. I foresaw a mutual coming together, an acceptance, an understanding of truth. Being a part of this new experience excited me.

❧ ❧ ❧ ❧

Later in the week, one of my Sunday-school-class members, concerned about me, contacted Patsy, our class president. Patsy shared with her what was troubling me as well as our pastor's request that I no longer teach.

She then wrote to me, saying that she and Patsy agreed to pray for me and that she was sorry that I was having a difficult time. She said she didn't understand and knew others could be cruel, but that the women in my class all sympathized with me and that she'd always be willing to talk with me.

Even if we hold different viewpoints, we can still be friends and agree to disagree.

Know that I still love you as a sister in Christ, just as I always did.

This was one of my sad days. I again awoke feeling sad and almost depressed, ready to cry at the least little thing. Another friend from church, with whom I'd recently had a long conversation, called me at least five times, concerned about me and seeming fearful that I might commit suicide. I understood why she was worried, as I had cried almost constantly as I shared my story with her.

❧❧❧❧

About a week later I drove to Austin to see Linda, my cousin from North Carolina, who was in the area visiting her son and his family. She's almost two years older than I, and as children, we spent much time together. As she and I talked one evening, the subject turned to children, their behaviors, and whether their behaviors are learned or inborn.

Linda, with three children of her own and a lifetime of experience caring for the children of others, stated, "I believe people are just born a certain way and that not all behavior is learned." As she pursued this line of thought, she told me her son-in-law's brother had died of AIDS. "I'm firmly convinced this young man couldn't help the fact that he was gay," she said.

"I totally agree with you," I replied. "I'm the same way."

Without responding verbally to my confession, she raised an eyebrow with a questioning look on her face.

"Yes, I'm gay."

She and I had no opportunity to share further until the next evening, when we went for a walk. Before we reentered the house, I asked, "Would you like to talk about my being gay? If you don't, I certainly understand."

"Yes, I would," she replied, so we remained outside as I told her my story. Although tears came to my eyes a few times, I never did cry, which convinced me I was making progress emotionally. Linda was very kind and receptive, which amazed me because she's been Southern Baptist all her life, and her parents were very strict. Once when we were children and playing a card game in her living room, her mother rushed in saying, "Put those cards away! Hurry, put those cards up! The preacher's walking up the sidewalk. I don't want him to see those cards!"

We quickly did as she asked, and I found the incident rather odd. My parents played cards often, especially canasta, so I'd never been taught that playing card games was of the devil. But Linda was brought up in a much more conservative atmosphere.

As she and I later headed to our separate bedrooms, I handed her copies of Jim's letter in which he wanted to know why I wanted the divorce, my reply to him in which I came out, and my pastor's letter to me. The next morning when she returned them to me, she simply thanked me for sharing. I was disappointed she made no comment as I yearned for her to ask questions, to show interest in what my life had been like, but I suppose she was reluctant to discuss the subject. Despite her belief that people didn't choose to be homosexual, I felt her religious background held her back from discussing such a forbidden subject.

☙☙☙☙

The following Wednesday evening, when I attended the church supper and prayer meeting, I sat at a table that included Carl Atkins, the fellow I'd been so catty and rude to three weeks earlier. Thank goodness he spoke and carried on a short conversation with me. Progress.

Several older women got my attention in order to compliment me on my handbell playing at the evening service. "How in the world do you play two bells in one hand?" they asked.

I just laughed and said something about it taking a lot of practice because you have to turn one bell one direction and the other another direction. I was pleased the members had a good impression of me.

Barbara also sat at the supper table with me and, in a private moment, said, "Mary Lou Reynolds approached Georgia Hunt (two church members about my age) asking if what she'd heard about you was true. Georgia told her it was. If Mary Lou's heard about it, you can assume everyone in that class knows or soon will."

This class was comprised of more than fifty women about my age. Their monthly class meeting was the next night, and I was invited as an associate member. Hearing Barbara's news caused me to lose courage and have cold feet about attending.

Upon returning home from church, I wrote Barbara.

When I invited Nancy Grayson to ride with me to tomorrow night's party, I didn't realize everyone would probably know about me. Do you think that she might prefer not to? Would you mind checking and seeing because I would certainly understand. I'm reaching the point where I feel I'm doing a friend a disservice for just the two of us to be together for fear others might say something about her. In fact, I've thought many times I may be soiling your reputation by sitting beside you as much as I do. I'm starting to feel that old pull toward going back and being the loner that I used to be.

Barbara replied the next day.

Just talked to Nancy. She says you're friends because she thinks you're a terrific person, and she doesn't care how many people know that. She just likes you. Both of us are enjoying a new freedom (for lack of a better word) in our friendship with you now that you aren't a committed loner anymore. We'd greatly prefer that you not crawl back in that hole. I can't imagine that being seen with you would damage my reputation in any way. (What does that generally is my shooting off my big mouth!)

❧ ❧ ❧ ❧

After returning from the party that night, I wrote a quick note to Barbara to tell her that everything went fine. However, I did get the feeling that several women were having trouble with the news, especially one of them. I glanced at her several times and found her staring at me, but as soon as she saw me looking, she averted her eyes. She also never spoke to me.

Barbara replied late in the evening that some people need time to deal with my news but will eventually find out that I'm exactly the same person now that I've always been, except more real. Her words calmed me, relieving some of my anxiety.

Chapter Twenty

Janie came by that Saturday to drive me to a wedding shower. Just when I thought I'd finally begun to control my emotions, I took one look at her and all those resolutions disappeared. My feelings swamped my logic, leaving me nauseated. I desired her beyond words, thankful that she seemed to enjoy having me for a friend. Surely I'd never do anything so foolish that she wouldn't want me around any more. That fear of making a fool of myself kept me alert whenever she was near.

≈≈≈≈≈

On Sunday, April 30, as soon as I returned home from church, I turned on CNN's live broadcast of the Gay Rights Rally in Washington, D.C. This was the first one I'd ever watched, and it impressed me. The speakers were neatly dressed, well groomed, and spoke intelligently. I'm not certain why I was afraid it might be otherwise, except that I was as misinformed about gays as everyone else was.

When the cameras zoomed in on same-sex couples openly showing affection for each other (a hand on a shoulder, two partners back-to-back slowly moving rhythmically together to music, some with arms loosely around each other), tears sprang to my eyes. I was unaware of this world, yet deep inside I'd always yearned for it.

How I envied these couples. I spent the afternoon watching the broadcast and occasionally wrote down statements that the speakers made. I loved what the mother of two gay children said: "Having a gay child is the ultimate test of unconditional love."

&⁊.&⁊.&⁊.&⁊

I continued to fantasize about Janie, and it was driving me nuts! I knew it was wrong, yet the forbidden enjoyment attached to it made me prolong my thoughts.

Several days later, on May 4, Janie called. "Lou Anne," she said, "Wilson Rhodes phoned me to ask if I would substitute as a teacher for our Sunday-school class. We ended up having a very long conversation, and I told him that it amazed me how everyone could respect you as an outstanding Christian one hour, and then the next, after you were honest, no longer thought of you in the same way."

As I listened to her, I realized she was saying that my honesty was my downfall. I thought immediately of the scripture that proclaimed the truth will set you free, but I knew that the freedom it referred to was an inward feeling and that I *was* truly free in that respect. Generally speaking, it was a wonderful state to be in, but my honesty about my sexual orientation had placed me in bondage, enslaved to the prejudices of others.

Janie repeated how she'd told Wilson I was the very best Sunday-school teacher she'd ever had, that all the class loved me and wanted me to remain as their teacher, and that if he considered me unworthy to teach, then everyone in the church was unworthy because she considered me one of the best Christians she'd ever known. She praised me up one side and down the other and said Wilson did admit he'd heard that I was a good teacher.

She also told him that I was so good that I even advised her not to sit beside me because people might think things about her that weren't true. But Janie said she planned to continue to sit by me, that she had a very good marriage of thirty-three years and loved her husband. "You need to know that Lou Anne is not hitting on any of the class members," she informed him.

Her words shocked me. "Did you really say that to him?"

"Yes, I did. That, and more."

"Did you actually use the term 'hitting?'"

"I did! I thought he ought to know you aren't doing something like that."

That idea had never occurred to me. Could anyone ever think I was that type of person? I wasn't even certain I knew what "hitting on someone" meant, but I surmised it implied making some type of sexual overture or suggestion.

I'd never had any desire to hit on anyone! In all those years since Karen and I parted, I'd never felt any desire toward a particular woman, other than my present infatuation with Janie, probably because I'd denied myself any close friendships over the years.

Now that I was consumed by desire for Janie, I found that many other emotions that had lain dormant over the years were peeking out from their hiding places. My heart was warming up, and I was learning to care for others in ways new to me. But these new feelings were scary. I felt unstable, almost dizzy in that I wasn't certain which way I needed to lean. I wanted to care for others, a characteristic Christian virtue. Caring, however, could also expose my heart to painful experiences such as hurt, heartbreak, anguish, and torment. Was it worth it? Wouldn't I be better off not feeling anything at all? Undeniably, YES, I would definitely be better off without experiencing emotions!

As all these thoughts flooded my mind, Janie repeatedly told me such things as, "Lou Anne, you're such a good person. I've never heard a bad word come out of your mouth."

Wanting to change the subject, I shared with her the fact that Patsy, our class president, was ill, and that I'd taken supper to her last night. "See," she said, "that's what I mean! You're such a good person!"

Again wanting to change the subject, I said, "Speaking of our class, I can't decide whether to join you on Sundays. If you have a substitute, I'm afraid I might make her feel uncomfortable, and I don't want to do that."

"That's what I mean, Lou Anne! You're just too good! You should certainly continue to come to our class. You won't make anyone feel uncomfortable."

Janie had me on some kind of pedestal I didn't deserve. When she'd decided to tell me about Wilson's phone call, she'd said, "I don't want us to have any secrets from each other."

She was so right, yet I continued to hide my feelings toward her. It would be a terrible mistake to tell her how much I was in love with her, but I supposed I should tell her the truth. However, just writing down these thoughts made me nauseous. I had to think about something else.

Janie did tell me that she'd called our departmental director to see if she'd talked with Wilson about me. She hadn't. "Does she know about me?" I asked Janie.

"Yes, Lou Anne, she knows. And she also told

me that quite a few in our department would not be at all accepting of you and what you are. She told me she could easily name several of them."

I immediately thought, "All the more reason to remain in that department, to be an example of a gay Christian."

☙ ☙ ❧ ❧

Sundays continued to be decision days. Which class should I attend? My old class or Barbara's? I was always being pulled from both sides, with Barbara repeatedly telling me to stay away from my old class. She was always writing me to that effect.

Please consider not attending your class for a while, I mean a minimum of three to six months. The people in that class who aren't comfortable with your situation can't express themselves freely so long as you're there, and they need to. Discussing it among themselves will work in your favor more strongly than your continued presence in the class/department will. Your feelings are involved in something stronger than a teacher/class relationship there, and this emotional pull creates a temptation/risk that could harm you permanently, not to mention the danger to your cause and the church body as a whole.

I confided to Barbara that I was in a hopeless situation regarding Janie.

I'm completely torn between wanting two different things that are completely incompatible, and it keeps me constantly torn up. I've heard that when you're in love you think of this other person up to 85 percent of the time.

I could relate to those statistics, although I did feel I was making progress. After all, I'd been in love with Janie for more than eight months. It was time to shake off my addiction, and, like an alcoholic, I was taking it just one day at a time. Sometimes even an hour at a time. But I could do it. I confided in Barbara about my determination.

At times I think I'm much improved, and then at other times I feel I'm reaching a very dangerous crossroads.

I was also aware that others might sense how I felt. It scared me, kept me in knots around Janie. Several times I'd come close to doing something that would have been so normal for me to do, like offering comfort to her in the form of a gentle touch or a holding of hands, actions that might possibly have raised eyebrows. At the last minute, my brain had kicked in and logic took over. But I had been almost shaking when I realized what a close call I'd experienced.

Past our normal bedtime, Barbara and I continued to write back and forth. She told me I was too close to my situation and that it was risky. She suggested that I make a list of the ways my life had improved in the past year, including my newfound freedom and privacy, and the challenge of setting my own goals.

She was right. I could ruin myself and my reputation, be useless in the cause I was determined to support, and harm my church. I had to keep these dangers uppermost in my mind at all times.

❧ ❧ ❧ ❧

I attended my second PFLAG meeting and thoroughly enjoyed it. The people there talked about their partners or their loves. I enjoyed their laughter, their humor, their friendliness toward each other, their openness, their Christianity.

That night all those who had attended the Millennium March in Washington, D.C. reported on their experiences, sharing many positives, such as the fact that the people who attended looked so normal. Very few far-out looking people were there, yet CNN interviewed and videoed the most bizarre-looking group of queens. According to the reports we heard at the meeting, the participants were friendly, kind, thoughtful, and considerate toward each other. They made a good impression on the citizenry who came in contact with them.

Our local participants carried signs such as, G O P (GUILTY OF PREJUDICE), I LOVE MY GAY SON UNCONDITIONALLY, and FOCUS ON YOUR OWN FAMILY. One of the members, who carried two of these signs, said that many, many people came up to her to ask if they could have their picture taken beside her sign (which said G O P on one side and UNCONDITIONALLY on the other). One fellow wanted his picture taken by the Unconditionally sign so he could send it to his mother for a Mother's Day gift. She hadn't contacted him for seven years. Obviously, she didn't love him unconditionally, and her rejection had devastated him.

The following afternoon I visited with Barbara for two hours. When I left she gave me a loaf of homemade bread. How I love homemade bread, especially with lots of butter! Yum, yum! I ended up eating three huge slices topped with fig preserves for supper. Delicious.

During our visit, Barbara alluded to a conversation she'd had about me with a male friend who thought I should talk to a psychologist to determine if I really was gay. "What did you say to him?" I asked.

I asked him, "You mean just like you did when you were a teenager and realized you liked girls?"

Barbara continued to urge me to find a counselor, which I was considering. I was definitely on the mend but continued to have great emotional upheavals.

Brenda, the woman I'd met at the PFLAG meeting the past month, sent me an e-mail telling me she'd just returned from a camping/canoeing trip to the Buffalo National River in Arkansas. I wrote her the following:

I envy you your trip! Sounds wonderful. By the way, I've been wanting to ask you a little more about what you do. One of my friends from church has been almost demanding that I find a counselor. I'm really doing much better but still fight some heavy emotional battles. That's probably to be expected, considering the drastic turn my life has taken. But maybe we could get together some day. I'm finally becoming able to talk without a box of tissues close at hand.

Brenda quickly replied.

The counseling I do these days is more of a ministry than an occupation. I'm trained in psychology (master's level) and biblical counseling, and certified as a pastoral counselor. I simply sit with folks, listen, and share whatever the Spirit lays on my heart. I'd be happy to sit with you some time, if you want. Tissues aren't an issue. I've gone through cases of them myself!
Take care, Brenda.

I was intrigued and wrote back.

I really would like to visit with you. I've never had an opportunity to share what has gone on in my life with another gay person.

Then I proceeded to tell her a little of my story before copying and pasting the two long letters Jim and I had sent to each other.

Along with writing to Brenda, I carried on quite a correspondence that day with Barbara and mentioned Brenda and her experience as a counselor.

As I wrote to Barbara, I reminded myself she was leaving for Italy the next afternoon and would be gone for three weeks. Janie was due back in Tyler in two days, would be here for only a week, then will leave on a ten-day trip to the Northeast. Just knowing they wouldn't be available had me already feeling nervous and lonely.

❧❧❧❧❧

One afternoon, when I went over to Mother's to balance her checkbook and review her finances, she shared with me the news of the death of one of her Little Rock friends who had been living with another woman after the death of her husband. Mother disapproved of their living arrangement, and today her criticism became harsher as she declared, "They are lesbians."

My heart lurched when she used the term lesbians, and in almost a combative tone I asked her, "Why would you say that?"

"People have actually seen them kiss each other on the lips."

Not knowing how to reply and not wanting to extend this conversation, I made no comment. An uneasy silence prevailed, and we dropped the subject.

Chapter Twenty-one

This morning I received an e-mail sent by someone who never sends me e-mails, but just calls instead. Janie! She was back in town and had bought a book, *How Good Do We Have To Be?*, to share with me.

I called her, and we visited for well over an hour before I attended my weekly Bible study.

That afternoon, I called her again to tell her I wanted to bring some papers over for her to read. The visit was going along fine until I admitted I was still experiencing a lot of pain and that the idea of climbing back into my hole looked very inviting.

Janie asked, "What's causing your pain?"

"I can't talk about it."

"Yes, you can. Tell me."

I became quiet, then said, "I can't talk to you about it."

"I know what's causing it. I've known for a long time, and it's time we talked about it."

I stood up and grabbed my purse. "I need to go. I can't stay any longer."

"You've got to stay and get this out in the open. You're in love with me, aren't you?"

By then I'd sat back down on the sofa. And at her revelation I bent over, touching my head to my knees, and began to wail, "Don't, don't, don't, please don't."

Janie began to rub my back, but I was shutting

everything out so I'm not even certain what she said. Something like, "Oh, Lou Anne. I've known about this for a long, long time. I'm just not inclined that way. I can't be in love with you like that."

"I know. I know. I've always known."

"I feel honored that you feel this way about me. You're such a wonderful person, so brilliant. Look at who you've fallen in love with. You're seeing me through rose-colored glasses."

"I have never seen you through rose-colored glasses. But you see me that way. I'm not brilliant."

"Lou Anne, what are we going to do? We've got to decide."

"I thought you'd never want to see me again once you found out how I feel about you."

"That's not true. You're my friend. I talk with you about things I don't discuss with anyone else. But if being with me brings you pain, we shouldn't be together any more."

At that point, I stood up and paced the room, first toward the door, then over to a front window, where I leaned my head against the glass. Then as I turned around to walk back to the sofa, I gave a little laugh and said, "I do feel a certain amount of relief in getting this out in the open."

"I know how painful love is, Lou Anne. I've been there."

"The despair isn't as great when I'm with you, Janie. I want to be your friend, but I just can't believe you'd want to be around me."

Janie took a deep breath. "You have to realize how long I've been aware of your feelings for me, yet all that time we've continued to be friends."

"But I don't want anyone to link your name to

mine. I don't want you to be hurt by being friends with me. Everyone will assume things about you, too."

"Yes. They already are!"

"What do you mean?"

"Don't kid yourself. People already think things like that, but it doesn't bother me. But if someone were to come up to me and say something, I'd just quit going to church."

"That's the wrong thing to do. That would convince them that what they said was true."

"I hadn't thought about that, but you're probably right. You have so much courage, and I don't. Who else knows about this?"

"Barbara. She guessed it."

"Laura knows, doesn't she?"

"Oh, no!"

"Laura's bound to know."

"I certainly hope not."

"Why does that bother you?"

"I just don't want her to know."

She gently rubbed my forearm with a couple of her fingers. "Your skin's as soft as a ten-year-old's. Oh, I just don't know what to say. Tell me what to do. Did I cause this?"

"No, you had nothing to do with how I feel."

"This happened a long time ago, didn't it?"

"In August. Yes, a long time ago. How long have you been aware of it?"

"In October, when you came back from your trip to Singapore. That's when I knew."

(I had taken Mother to Singapore to visit my brother and his family, who were living there for a year. That's when I chose a beautiful blue silk fabric as a gift for Janie, who is an expert seamstress.)

"Over seven months ago. Janie, you've known that long?"

"Yes."

"I'm too old for this, Janie. I'm feeling things that teenagers feel."

"It's because you didn't have an opportunity to date normally."

"You're right. I'm totally inexperienced."

At this point in our conversation, Janie named several female couples, heterosexuals, who took trips together every summer. This was news to me. "No one thinks anything about it," she said. "And my good friend, Lisa, who now has Alzheimer's, she and I used to walk down the street together and into stores together hand-in-hand. People won't think things about you and me."

"Oh, but they will, because I'll be labeled as gay and whoever I'm with will have that label too."

"Well, it just doesn't bother me. Lou Anne, you've got to promise me you'll contact the woman from PFLAG and talk with her. Don't you really want to?"

"Yes, a part of me does."

"I think she's reaching out to you in kindness, and you need to be willing to talk with her. If something develops between the two of you, that would be great. But you've got to open yourself up to new relationships. You really need to find someone to be with. You've got a lot of years left, and you don't want to spend them all alone."

I promised. As she walked me out to my car, I could tell she was undecided about giving me the usual hug when we departed. By keeping a lot of distance between us, I let her know it wasn't at all necessary, and she almost took me up on it. But at the last minute, she said, "Give me a hug, Lou Anne." And I did.

As we said good-bye, Janie said, "Call me, Lou Anne. I want you to call me."

"You just don't know what a game I play with myself as to how long I can go without phoning you."

"You can phone me every day if you like. That'd be just fine. If you don't, I'll be calling you! I love you!"

"I love you too." And I drove away marveling at what a turn my life had taken. I was amazed, overwhelmed that my most private secret was now out in the open to Janie. But how foolish I'd been to assume she wasn't aware of my feelings for her. How dumb I was! How many others could see the truth? I hated to even think about it.

Chapter Twenty-two

When the phone rang early the next morning, I knew it had to be Janie. No one else called me this early. She'd written me two long e-mails and lost them.

After a few minutes of conversation about how she had known I was in love with her, I said, "Janie, do you believe love has to come from God?"

"Yes, I do. It can't come from the devil. I don't even believe lust comes from the devil. If it weren't for lust, we wouldn't have procreation."

"Janie, you are different." We both laughed.

"Yes, I am, precious."

"I just wish I could get over this, that it wouldn't last much longer."

"Well, sometimes it can take a long, long time."

"That doesn't give me much hope!"

"You need to meet someone that you can have for a partner, to share life with. I really want that for you. Right now, you're in some kind of adolescent stage, going through things that you should have experienced a long time ago."

Wanting to change the subject, I said, "Janie, I know you and Charles tell each other everything, but I'd feel very uncomfortable for him to know I've fallen in love with you."

"I haven't told him, precious. This is just between the two of us."

Toward the end of our conversation, Janie said, "You have to promise me that if our friendship brings you too much pain, you'll tell me."

"I promise."

After we hung up, I began thinking about a Ted Loder meditation that reads, "Expose my shame where it shivers, crouched behind the curtains of propriety, until I can laugh at last through my common frailties and failures, laugh my way toward becoming whole."

My shame, falling in love with Janie, had now been exposed, a shame I'd hidden for almost a year. How foolish I was to think that I was actually protecting a secret that to Janie wasn't a secret at all. The situation now looked so absurd there was no other possible reaction but to laugh at the senselessness of hiding the truth.

I was in a state of shock following Janie's revelation. I'd lost my appetite again and didn't sleep much, thinking, thinking, thinking of Janie's knowing I was in love with her. I felt shattered at my inability to keep my feelings to myself and devastated that she'd known for such a long time. What a fool I'd probably made of myself. Yet part of me was overwhelmingly grateful for her friendship and her willingness to continue it. That truly amazed me and made me feel quite humble.

Could I continue to look her in the eye? The things I'd thought about us made me ashamed. Over and over I could hear Janie say, "I know the source of your pain, Lou Anne. I've known it for a long, long time."

I began thinking of the devastation I'd brought down on myself and my life. Many people experienced life-changing tragedies such as the death of their spouse or child, loss of a job, the destruction of their home, or bleakness from some tragic illness, but these had some outward cause. What had happened to me was an inwardly based misery, one I should have been able to control, but I couldn't.

My well-ordered, well-structured life had crumbled. It was no more. And what I was left with was the shell of a person I didn't even think I knew. There'd been a death in my family, and it'd been me. I was gone.

Why had I fallen in love with Janie? How many times had I asked myself that question, over and over and over? Why?

Why Janie? Who else? I had no friends, just acquaintances. That's all Janie was. Just an acquaintance. A member of the Sunday-school class I taught. But I saw in her something special, something different. She was kind, loving and tenderhearted toward all people, even those who were different. I fell in love with Janie because she was a good person, someone I enjoyed being around, someone with whom I could talk.

That's the way it was with Karen. We had loved to talk and share thoughts and feelings. And speaking of Karen, my feelings for her had practically disappeared. I suppose they really had disappeared. I was curious about what I'd feel toward her if we were to see each other. But when I thought of who I would most prefer to be with, I had no doubt whatsoever. Janie.

When I allowed myself the freedom to dream, to fantasize about her, I felt bodily reactions—a hollowness within me followed by a type of constriction in my chest and then this pain. I had to get over this. I couldn't continue to live with my sinful desires. I didn't allow myself to fantasize nearly as much as I used to. This was a good sign, I thought.

This new setback, Janie's knowing that I was in love with her, had really thrown me. Was I that transparent? I was amazed that the thoughts of suicide hadn't started entering my mind on a regular basis. Really amazed. Could I continue to keep those thoughts at bay?

Soon after lunch, I e-mailed Janie and told her she'd done absolutely nothing she shouldn't have. Actually, I said, I didn't think *I* had done anything I shouldn't have. I also told her I felt ashamed, embarrassed, and humiliated and pondered constantly what was really happening to me. Was what I was going through truly a part of God's plan for my life, or was the devil having a field day tormenting me? I was drawn more to that second thought.

$$\mathcal{N}\mathcal{N}\mathcal{N}$$

Just before supper that evening, I received an e-mail from my brother Tom, who said that Mom had called last week and, among many other things, asked if he'd heard from me and if I knew what was going on. He took back his recommendation that I not tell her what was up with me.

He said Mom had apologized for being so critical of his friendliness with Warren, one of our relatives who is gay, and wondered if her reconsideration had come from something I'd said to her.

He also said that if I was politically and publicly active in Tyler, she would eventually hear something and be more upset about being excluded than anything else.

Though he rescinded his previous recommendation, he didn't have a new one except to arrange for her to think all the family was being informed at the same time.

I immediately replied that I had no idea what was

going on with Mother, especially the apology concerning his friendship with Warren.

She had recently told me that she felt she was a millstone around my neck and apologized repeatedly for thinking I had another man in my life. She also said she regretted not supporting me when Jim and I first thought about divorcing.

I also told Tom that Mother seemed to be seeing through me because I'd been reluctant to sit down and visit with her about anything, afraid she would bring up the subject I didn't want to think about.

Then I ended my note to Tom on a new, more positive note.

Tonight I'm stepping out into something new for me. I've attended two PFLAG meetings and met a woman experienced in counseling. We're going to meet in less than an hour. I definitely need some counseling, but I'm uncertain this is the route I should go. However, this new step I am taking is an opportunity to actually talk to another gay. I've never done that before.

Brenda's small home was about ten minutes away by car. As I perched on her sofa while, off to the side, she relaxed in a stuffed chair, I told her everything. We visited from six thirty until almost nine p.m. Although I didn't bawl like I had in the past, I used a bunch of tissues. When I told her that I felt like I had a brick cylinder inside me that had developed a crack and allowed my emotions to begin to escape, she liked that analogy. She said she'd always used the idea of a bucket that finally becomes so full of emotion it begins to spill over—based on the theory that we're able to contain only so much emotion before it has to escape.

When I completed my story, Brenda asked, "Do you want advice?"

"Yes, please."

"I wouldn't tell your mother about your sexual orientation. She may not want to know. Tell her only if she asks."

Then she asked, "Do you realize that you and Janie have no future?"

"Yes. I've always known that."

"You know that you and Janie can never have a physical relationship?"

"Yes. I've got to get over my feelings for her."

"Then whenever you begin fantasizing about Janie, picture yourself walking along a beach with Jesus by your side. Every time the thought of Janie pops into your mind, force yourself to picture the beach scene."

"At last!" I thought. "Some sensible guidance. Something that just might work." I was ready to grab whatever reasonable advice was offered to end my nine-month-long misery. A beautiful, sandy beach with waves gently lapping the shore has always been a pleasant, peaceful scene for me. And to be walking in tandem with Jesus, the epitome of love and acceptance, would make the vision idyllic. Yes, this was something I could do.

"You said you cry and feel sad and aren't certain why," Brenda pointed out. "It's important that you focus on what's making you cry. Identify the cause. If you think you don't know, take a guess. Your best guess is your best answer. Grieve over that particular thing. You'll never be able to fill up what you call your empty shell until you've grieved through all the issues causing the tears. And you can't do that until you identify them—which can be very difficult."

Before I left, she suggested that sometime we

should go out for pizza together or something like that. Brenda is eleven years younger than I am. Her former husband didn't know she's gay, but her sons and her mother did.

≈≈≈≈

It had been almost six full days since Janie told me she knew the source of my pain and five days since I'd heard from her. I fell into despair and kept telling myself to just survive. That was my only goal for the day. I wanted so badly to die. I finally left the apartment and rented four videos. I had to just stay alive all day. That's all. Just live.

≈≈≈≈

Early the next day, Janie called. I couldn't believe it! And she sounded like her old self as she shared with me all the house problems she'd been going through. When she heard my hesitating voice as I said hello to her, she asked, "Lou Anne, is anything wrong?"

"I just thought you didn't want to talk with me anymore."

"Oh, no, no! Not at all."

And off our conversation went. My heart was so much lighter.

≈≈≈≈

Both Barbara and Janie were out of town, and I started communicating with Brenda by e-mail, asking her questions about herself, to which she replied.

I, like you, have lived most of my life in the box of safety and meeting others' expectations. Only in the last three years or so have I begun to truly know and live from my adventurous spirit.

After sharing information about some trips she'd taken, she answered my question as to which church she attended.

Right now I worship on Sunday mornings at St. Gabriel's Community Church, a small evangelical, nondenominational gay-friendly church here in Tyler. Since my summer in Wyoming, I view church in a different way than I once did. I'll share with you sometime.

Hope you have a good day! Brenda

❧❧❦❦

Barbara was home. Janie probably was too, but she hadn't contacted me.

❧❧❦❦

Days passed and I wasn't in the mood to write or to do anything. What a struggle life was. Janie hadn't called or written. Nothing. She could have been ill, or have had a family emergency, or something could have happened to her parents, but still I pictured her here in Tyler choosing not to contact me. How was I going to stand not ever visiting with her again? Not ever seeing her again. I was in total misery.

Knowing Barbara had returned, I shared with her all that had been going on, especially my conversation with Janie in which she admitted having known the source of my pain for many months. Several days before, I'd also informed Barbara of my contacts with Brenda and of her advice, as well as emphasizing how highly I thought of her and how much I valued her friendship.

Brenda's advice sounds terrific—grounded in faith, pragmatic (I hate pie-in-the-sky advice), and positive. Next time you see her, tell her about your sleeping problem (if you haven't) and see what she thinks. That concerns me, especially right now when I am sleep-deprived myself and know how it feels.

Your mother may already know as much as she wants to. Using a mental image of beach-walking with Jesus to substitute for thoughts of Janie is a positive suggestion, it seems to me. Have you tried to identify specific things that draw you to Janie? Obviously, the attraction is primarily physical, but I think there's more, and maybe part of it is Janie's openness about her emotions, which is something you haven't allowed yourself to experience. Perhaps when you recognize what that part of the attraction is, you'll be better able to recognize those qualities in someone else. (Remember, I'm a journalism major, not a therapist, so give any suggestion I make all the attention it deserves!) I think you'll be able to identify the cause(s) for the tears as time goes on, too.

Raining, and I want to turn the computer off. Don't talk too nice to me. Makes me think you've heard that I have a terminal illness.

Barbara made me chuckle as I thought about why I was drawn to Janie, and I attempted to express my theories.

My attraction isn't physical. If it had been physical, I would have been attracted to her when I first met her. But we were acquaintances for a year before I fell in love with her.

Pure meanness on the part of God? Oh, I've considered that possibility many times. I don't think I deserved this. And I feel anger and sometimes hate and sometimes just sorrow when I think of God doing this to me. If I'd done something I shouldn't have, I could say I deserved what I got. But I played the game by the only rules I knew. And even though they hurt me all the time, I stuck with them. I denied myself a chance to be happy, and you'd think I'd receive something positive for my efforts instead of this agony I'm experiencing. It's as if the world has turned upside down and I'm powerless to make it right.

But I'm digressing. What attracted me to Janie? Probably learning of her openness and acceptance of homosexuals. What a bombshell to have someone sit and talk with me about a subject I'd always refused to bring into consciousness and to have that person verbally demonstrate love, kindness, and acceptance toward people I'd always been taught were abominable. Who would have thought a Christian existed who displayed a loving acceptance toward homosexuals?

A recent television special called Love Chronicles *stated that we all have a certain chemistry, so when we meet an individual under intense conditions, we're drawn to them: hence my attraction to Janie.*

I gave Barbara more information I'd gleaned from the television special, then copied that letter and forwarded it to Brenda, who quickly replied.

From my experience, both in what I have learned professionally and through personal experience, all of your explanations for your attraction to Janie are certainly as reasonable as anything in the realm of love can be.

We're attracted to individuals who manifest those qualities that we haven't recognized or nurtured within ourselves. For women, physical attraction is usually not the primary force behind attraction. The emotional attraction is far greater. The circumstance of the meeting is certainly a factor. The more intense the situation, the greater the emotional bonding that occurs.

Brenda's affirmation of my explanations brightened my day just a little, though it was so dark that I saw only a glimpse of light. She said she planned to attend the gay-pride parade in Houston that weekend with some friends from the gay community in Tyler. They were all younger, with partners, and Brenda admitted that at times she missed the company and friendship of someone nearer her age and not in a relationship, who could identify with her experiences of long-term marriage and children. She hadn't found many single, fifty-plus-year-old lesbians freely walking around in Tyler, Texas.

Lou Anne, as you express your appreciation for my staying in touch and offering friendship, in all honesty, I also appreciate you.
May you have a peaceful night's rest! Psalm 4:8.
Brenda

The next afternoon, after my regular checkup, I replied to Brenda, telling her that I'd dropped so much weight I now wore a size 5 instead of a 10 or 12, as I had before this stressful period in my life began. The doctor had put me on Prozac, but I couldn't comprehend how a medicine could help a depressed person when I knew my depression was an emotional response to my situation. I'd had a horrible week worrying why Janie hadn't called.

The only gay women I know are the few I've met at the PFLAG meetings. There's not another gay woman in Tyler that I know of.

I envy young gay women. To have the courage to come out when you're young would be wonderful. I never felt that option was available. But after this awful experience with Janie, and the painful emotions that keep me tied up in knots, I'm never again going to fall in love. It's pure misery.

I think the time has come for you to tell me a little more about yourself. So far, our friendship has centered on my problems. Rather a selfish situation on my part. So tell me something I don't know about you, maybe how you met your husband, why you married him, or something. Were you ever in love with him?

Brenda wrote back that my doctor should have explained how Prozac could help me. She said I was apparently clinically depressed because of the lengthy duration of my emotional stress, which had slowed the chemical processes in my brain. She compared the mishap to a four-cylinder engine that had begun to hit on only two or three cylinders. The Prozac should jump-start my brain, she assured me, which helped me understand what was happening to me.

Then she told me a little about herself.

I started dating my ex-husband between my junior and senior year in high school. He was six years older. I was the intelligent, competent, most-likely-to-succeed valedictorian of a small high school. I went to a fairly large university right out of high school only to discover that I was shy, insecure, lonely, and had no sense of my own identity outside the roles I maintained in small-town USA. Of course, this is all from a backward glance.

Brenda asked me out for a light dinner Friday evening so we could continue swapping stories. That sounded like fun, and I looked forward to the opportunity to visit with her further and to learn more of her story, which I felt was still mostly untold.

Though I'd enjoyed my conversation with Brenda, the next day was no better. I was terribly depressed, down in that very deep hole. All I did was lie around, cry, and do lots of nothing. This was my second day on the Prozac, and it certainly hadn't shown any signs of helping me.

Chapter Twenty-three

When Barbara wrote the next morning, asking how I was feeling, I confessed that I thought Janie might be wanting to end our friendship. She replied that Janie would just tell me if that's what she wanted to do.

Please, if you go into a funk, let it be one that you enter on a somewhat realistic basis, and not one you slide into on the basis of imagination alone. Work on imagining something wonderful you'd have to cope with. Emotions are notoriously unreliable indicators of truth.

She asked if I'd been able to exercise any and recommended it. And she also suggested that a Dairy Queen Butterfinger Blizzard might taste good to me.

You're going to be well, and you're going to truly enjoy your life again before this year is over—and, quite possibly, before this month is over. I'm glad you're going to see Brenda, and I'm glad it'll be in a restaurant.

I thanked her for the encouraging words about Janie.

I tell myself old women aren't supposed to have feelings like this. I know that just accepting the fact that I'm gay is a big enough jump for you, but to even begin to fathom my being in love with another woman must stretch anyone's limits of understanding! Thanks for not preaching to me about it, but just guiding me. I need that.

Eating Blizzards is a good idea. That always sounds good. Heath Bar is my favorite.

I assured her that I usually walked about an hour every day and normally performed various exercises for about twelve minutes each morning, but that had been going by the wayside. When I walked, I usually kept a little notebook with me that contained all the poems and Biblical chapters I'd memorized and I mentally recited them. But I hadn't done that lately because I couldn't focus for long stretches of time.

Barbara quickly replied.

Having accepted that you're gay (which took about 35 seconds, since it explained quite a few things), I have no difficulty accepting your being in love. I do have a problem (as I'm sure you've noticed) understanding why it makes you a touch irrational from time to time. Please feel free to call me on my own periodic fits of irrationality!

I laughed at her reply, realizing how nutty I am when it comes to Janie. What a blessing to have an intelligent friend like Barbara who saw through my crazy thoughts and bravely expressed her opinion. Still, even though I knew I was being foolish, I continued to believe Janie was deliberately avoiding me, and I wallowed in despondency.

❧❧❧❧❧

Three days later, Barbara wrote that she hadn't

heard a word from me and wanted to know if I was okay. She asked me to talk to her about something, so I dumped my concerns on her.

I quickly replied that Janie hadn't been in Sunday school or at a wedding in the afternoon. Several people had asked where she was, but I hadn't heard from her for nineteen days. My emotions were roller-coastering, though at least I didn't stay down for three or four days in a row. If I did, I wouldn't still be around.

Several of my class members approached me Sunday and told me they all thought I needed to return to the class as a member. It's nice to be wanted. Since I like being with them so much, it's quite a temptation.

Brenda and I had a good visit at Jason's Deli. We have much in common since she was married for twenty years and has two sons. She also understands the pain I'm going through with Janie because she's experienced something similar. She advocates complete separation from Janie, a suggestion you would heartily endorse.

Barbara wrote back, asking if she could meet Brenda sometime, saying that she sounded like a person actively involved in figuring out life and helping others do the same.

She also said that, based on personal experience, she doubted I could return to my class without teaching and urged me to wait at least six months before I decided what to do.

I wouldn't wish what you're going through right now on my worst enemy, but I'm learning to know you so much better, Lou Anne. And I like that, as I'd always believed I would. You have so many strengths, and right now you're feeling so weak. I wonder if realizing how little control any of us really has over our lives is a prerequisite to experiencing the reality of God in a new and powerful way?

Barbara, above all others, knew of my many weaknesses and failures as a human being, so when she indicated that she recognized my strengths, I felt uplifted, renewed. And she was certainly right about God being more real, more vital, more loving when a person is at their weakest.

❧❧❧❧

I wrote to Barbara the next night that I'd swallowed my pride and called Janie. Her husband, Charles, had answered and explained that Janie was touring Texas with a friend visiting here for the first time. He expected her back the next night. He sounded very friendly, which relieved me considerably, as I'd feared he might know of my feelings toward Janie.

Barbara's answer made me smile.

I read this two or three times and considered not saying, "Told you so!" But I'm weak. So...told you so.

❧❧❧❧

I awoke feeling better. Usually I could tell within a few minutes of when I got up what kind of day I'd probably have, which amazed me. No tears at all! And no effort all day to keep them away. I was starting to hear the bugles of the cavalry riding to my rescue.

❧❧❧❧

Janie called, (it had been three weeks since I'd spoken to her), and we had a nice long conversation about what was going on in both our lives.

❧❧❧❧

Day eleven of taking the Prozac, and I'd had no tears for three or four days. Amazing! What a change.

I spent all yesterday afternoon chauffeuring Greg, a wheelchair-bound friend whose wife was in my former Sunday-school class. I assumed he knew I was gay, but I was wrong. That's when I discovered how much more difficult it was for me to out myself to a male. His reactions were so different!

"I'll take you to a gay bar," he said, "so you can have a good time. I'll even pretend to be gay myself, which shouldn't be too hard since I'll be sitting in this wheelchair." He eventually said, "All you need is to have a good romp in bed. That'd get you over your depression."

Greg didn't know very much about homosexuality and thought I was just mixed up. Our conversation covered various topics. He was surprised to learn I'd asked for the divorce. He was unaware, almost shocked, that Dr. Watson had asked me to take a sabbatical from teaching my Sunday-school class after I'd confided in him. The unfairness of it floored Greg—that my sharing a confidence had led to what might be conceived as a punishment.

❧❧❧❧

The Prozac made me feel different. No tears, but more than that, I didn't feel any emotion of any kind. Sterile might be a good word to describe it.

When I attended Sunday school, I spotted Janie in my former Sunday-school department directly across a wide hallway. My heart started racing. I hadn't seen her for three and a half weeks. I immediately turned and walked into my new department to avoid her seeing me, as I didn't think I could properly handle our greeting each other.

When classes were over, I spotted her again as she visited with friends in the other department. Still wanting to avoid her, I headed straight for the staircase despite my yearning to speak with her. She looked gorgeous. I had to garner all my willpower to head down the stairs. However, when I reached my car, I decided to sit there and wait for her to reach the parking lot. After a short wait, I spotted her coming in my direction. At that point, I got out and called to her when she was only a few cars away.

Seeming excited to see me, she hurried over and greeted me with a hug. "How are you doing, precious? It's been ages since I've seen you."

We stood beside my car and visited for about ten minutes, and Janie was as friendly as ever. "Give me a call and let's meet for lunch some day this week," she said.

Her invitation relieved me; she still considered me a good friend. But I knew I'd never call her and set a date. Nevertheless, her words were welcome, and I couldn't help but hope she might phone me.

❧❧❧❧

That evening at the church service, Barbara and her husband sat beside me. I really appreciated that. At one point in the service, as members of the congregation were passing the peace, she gave me a hug and even drew my cheek up next to hers. That surprised me and felt so good. Not only did it feel good, but she was very brave to hug a lesbian in front of the entire church. Had she thought through what she did? Later, I wrote to her to express my appreciation for her action, calling her courageous.

Oh my, I'm about to erase a momentary perception of myself as courageous. When I'm near someone I care about and we're passing the peace, I often hug that person afterward. Men and women, I touch people I love—what can I say? I hugged you because I wanted to express joy and togetherness and claim our mutual identity as God's dearly loved children. I've called you friend since I first met you, you know, and nothing has happened to change that. I don't expect it will.

No guts, no courage. Hate to disillusion you. I do have a few good qualities that I will trust you to recognize accurately as we go along.

❧❧❧❧

Brenda and I attended the July 4 outdoor band concert in the park. Sitting in our lawn chairs at the side of the outdoor amphitheater, we had a perfect view of both the band and the audience. Just prior to the start of the concert, I spied a couple walking toward some seats about halfway back. I thought, that surely does look like Janie and Charles, but she looks so young. I kept debating if it really was them or wondering if I was just wanting it to be Janie. But as I kept watching, and having a very difficult time paying attention to Brenda's conversation, I became increasingly convinced it really was Janie and Charles.

By then my heart was pounding like a trip-hammer, my stomach was in knots, and I got a hollow feeling in my chest. She was absolutely beautiful. I kept staring, hoping she'd look my way, but she didn't. Her long, blond hair hung down straight instead of being all frizzy. The summery red-and-white dress she wore made her look like a teenager. She and Charles looked fashionable while most of us were wearing shorts or jeans. When they sat down, I looked back and caught Charles's attention but never did see Janie look at me. She eventually shifted her position to where I couldn't even see her.

After the concert, when I noticed them walking in the other direction, I turned that way as I asked Brenda, "Would you like to meet Janie?"

"Not particularly," Brenda replied.

At that, I knew I'd be making a mistake to pursue the meeting, so, with a sick feeling in the pit of my stomach, I went with Brenda toward her home. I so wanted to say "Hi" to Janie.

When Barbara and I corresponded that evening, I told her that Brenda agreed to the three of us having lunch on Saturday. Both of these women were important to me, and I wanted Barbara to see that Brenda was a good person, trustworthy. When I had first told Barbara that I planned to meet with Brenda, she had warned me that Brenda might be a lesbian who would take advantage of me. I was aware of her concern and felt certain that once she met Brenda, all her fears would be allayed.

Chapter Twenty-four

The two-hour lunch yesterday with Barbara and Brenda was very pleasant. Because they both grew up in Kilgore (about thirty miles southeast), they had much in common to talk about. Later, Barbara wrote,

> *I enjoyed visiting with Brenda a lot, and would have liked her if I'd just met her somewhere without your involvement at all. Remember I'd suggested the possibility of an emotional involvement with her, and you said she was way too young? Well, it crossed my mind that there's about the same difference in your ages that there is between my sister and her husband. Brenda's not that young, especially considering her maturity. You two may never have an emotional attachment, but if not, it would be because the chemistry wasn't there, not because of her age.*

At our monthly PFLAG meeting, the president of the Dallas chapter spoke. When his son had told him and his wife that he was gay, they'd been stunned. They had no inkling their son had a different sexual orientation. After the initial shock wore off, they accepted him as he is and had since become strong supporters and advocates of gay rights. Interesting.

Brenda was unable to attend, so I called afterward to ask how she was. A bond was developing between us, yet I felt no emotional pull toward her. I wish I did. At times, however, I yearned for a closeness with someone.

❧ ❧ ❧ ❧

When Jim and I had lived in Austin, a couple named Corinna and Ed lived next door. Their children and ours freely moved between our homes and yards as her two sons were the same ages as our three boys, and even though Corinna was ten years younger than I, she had a grandson the age of Laura. I enjoyed having her family live next door to us.

One day I decided to out myself to her by sending the long, all-important letters Jim and I wrote to each other when we first discussed our divorce. Not long afterward, when I happened to be in Austin, I contacted her. She invited me to her home for a visit, where we enjoyed a good conversation during which I felt she accepted my being gay with no reservations.

In August, Corinna wrote that she was so glad I'd told her my story, because that was the way, one by one, our society might come to accept homosexuality as just another way to be. She'd told a couple of her friends, without mentioning names, and it made them think about the subject in a different way—as if I were someone close to them. Little by little, these conversations would make a difference, she said.

At times I felt as if I was just twiddling my thumbs and accomplishing nothing, so Corinna's letter was a bright spot, which I shared with Barbara.

My life had really been hectic, and perhaps that was good. Six days in Houston caring for my newborn grandson and six days in Austin helping my daughter settle into her new apartment. Then company in my apartment for two days. Added to that were my mother's health problems. My, My, My!

❧❧❧❧

Barbara wrote that she was rereading a book and for some reason found herself in the chapter called Testimony, which discusses testimony as an important part of the healing taking place all over the world through Alcoholics Anonymous.

The practice of testimony requires a person to commit voice and body to the telling of the truth. It guards the integrity of personal and communal life, as much on the grand stage of history as in the small exchanges of home. Today, living in a world where falsehood is strong, we need to support one another as we rise to bear witness, speaking the truth about what we have seen and heard.

Barbara said that the testimony most effective in her own life had been that shared in the context of living that life, the testimony given in order to maintain a relationship, the testimony required in the context of community. She said that my kind of testimony moved and changed her more than the public testimony of others did.

I thanked her for sharing these thoughts and confessed that I didn't speak to more people because I was afraid the subject might upset them, cause them discomfort and embarrassment.

Barbara replied that I'd know when to speak to individuals, though I might cry occasionally when I did. Her next comments intrigued me.

*I'm not sure self-control is all it's cracked up to be.
Maybe we need to know we're vulnerable and human,
and maybe other people need to know that about us, too.*

I had struggled all my life to maintain self-
control to protect myself. Now I was learning that being
vulnerable and showing emotion is more a reflection of
my humanity and authentic self than controlling myself.

❦❦❦❦

I attended a Sunday-school departmental party,
one with at least fifty people, and we had a great time
eating, visiting, and playing games. I was glad I went.

Though I knew I was out to many in this group,
I had no idea how many. Consequently, I felt rather
nervous walking in and immediately looked around for
Barbara but didn't see her. She was eating in another
room. When we began gathering for fellowship and
games, Barbara spotted me, came over, and gave me a
hug.

Upon returning home, I wrote to her that more
than one pair of eyes kept watching us when she greeted
and visited with me. And that wasn't my imagination
working overtime. She was hurting her reputation
by being so friendly to me, I warned her. Perhaps we
shouldn't sit together when around others. We didn't
need to raise eyebrows and instigate questions that
should never be raised.

When she didn't respond to this e-mail, I
eventually cornered her about it. She said that she'd
asked her husband if he'd noticed anything, and he said
he didn't. She then asked another friend if she'd spotted
anything, and the friend seemed amazed that Barbara

had even asked such a question.

After that, I decided not to poll the whole department!

I loved the way Barbara so often made me laugh at myself and by doing so urged me to not take my day-to-day concerns so seriously.

❧ ❧ ❧ ❧

I wrote Barbara that Brenda had come over the night before. This was the first time she'd been to my apartment, yet we'd met four and a half months earlier. She picked up supper for us and brought a video from the library for us to watch.

I felt quite odd about the evening, asking myself if this was what others would term a date. Yet we never touched each other. If a man had been visiting instead of a woman, he would probably have made a move of some kind. The idea of sitting close to her, just enjoying the physical nearness of another person, appealed to me, but we kept our distance. Later, after she left, I asked myself why homosexuals are perceived to be promiscuous.

Barbara replied that she was glad Brenda and I had a quiet, pleasant evening and that I was due one. As to my question about people's perception of gays as promiscuous, she thought part of it was the behavior of those in the public eye, such as Anne Heche and Ellen. Also part of it could be the number of intimate sexual relationships so many gays seemed to have before finding a partner to commit to, though tons of heterosexuals also had a number of sexually intimate relationships before marriage.

She said it sounded like Brenda and I were friends at this point, which was different from dating, that it depended on the emotions involved. She wasn't surprised that I longed for emotional closeness and the comfort of touch after such a rough few weeks, even months. Everyone needed it in some form or other, she reminded me.

Heterosexual women often hug each other, hold each other, in times of emotional stress. You never have— but most of us do.

From what little I know of her, Brenda's a neat person, a grown-up. Maybe you should just enjoy her company and not kill yourself analyzing stuff. If something develops between you, time enough then to analyze.

❧ ❧ ❧ ❧

Barbara wrote later that she'd reread what she'd written about gays being viewed as promiscuous and had more thoughts on the subject.

People who identify themselves publicly as gay don't have a great track record for commitment, and since they're just about the only gays people are aware of, that's what they assume. The commitment level of most people who seek public attention (actors, sports figures, whoever) isn't that dependable whether they're gay or not, but we know so many heterosexual people in our everyday lives who are faithful that we don't make that same assumption to the same degree. Thanks for being patient with me when my mouth outruns my brain. (After all, I'm only 64!)

࿇࿇࿇࿇

Janie and I rarely talked any more, but one day we spent over an hour on the phone catching up. I continued to miss her constantly.

࿇࿇࿇࿇

Late that afternoon Brenda and I joined a group of about twenty from St. Gabriel's for a Labor Day pool party held at the home of a female couple. Relaxing among this friendly group was just what I needed. Most of us stayed in the pool to find relief from the blazing sun. This was my first gay/lesbian party, and I felt as if I'd entered a different world. Actually, I *had* entered a different world.

Most of the crowd consisted of couples, who enjoyed the freedom to show affection toward their partners. Alcohol was available, and I wasn't accustomed to parties with alcohol. I'd led a very sheltered life and stuck to my soft drinks.

Toward evening, some of the women began to lose their inhibitions—due to the alcohol, I assumed. One couple, with arms around each other, shared a hammock. Feeling a touch of envy, I kept letting my eyes stray in their direction. Other couples in the pool occasionally kissed. The backyard was fenced, providing privacy, and these couples who normally had to hide their fondness for each other in public places were free in this setting to express their affection openly. Yes, it was a different world I had entered this afternoon and evening—and I liked it.

That change, however, was short-lived, as the

Sunday-school lesson the next morning dealt with perhaps the most famous of the infamous "six Biblical passages" condemning homosexuality, which was included in the broader lesson of Romans 1:18-32. Barbara never touched on the subject of homosexuality until her concluding statement, when she explained she had no time to discuss that part of the passage. She then handed out her Lesson Leftovers that she regularly shared at the end of each lesson—information she didn't have time to discuss with the class. Her leftovers included, among other things, *Views of Some Texas Baptist Leaders on Homosexuality*, which had been distributed at the Baptist General Convention in 1999.

> *Russell H. Dilday, Jr., president, BGCT (Baptist General Convention of Texas):*
> *According to the Bible, God's ideal for sex in marriage is one man, one woman in a monogamous relationship for life. Any divergence from ideal is contrary to God's will and therefore sinful. Homosexual practice is a perversion of God's plan and is described in the Bible as an abominable sin. Of course, there are other perversions, such as adultery and premarital sex, which the Bible also condemns as sexual sins.*
> *David Currie, director, Texas Baptists Committed:*
> *Homosexual activity is sinful as I understand the written word of God. Practicing homosexuals should not be elected leaders, nor should persons practicing greed, hatred, anger and prejudice (as a lifestyle) be church leaders. The church must balance Christ's call and example of treating sinners with grace and love while affirming biblical morality and the truth that things are clearly right and wrong.*

Phil Lineberger, president BGCT 1990-91:

I do not believe homosexual activity is natural or biblically acceptable, but I do believe people who have these tendencies need to be treated with respect as human beings created in the image of God.

Phil Strickland, director, Texas Baptist Christian Life Commission:

I believe that the Bible teaches that homosexual practice is inconsistent with Christian living. The Bible teaches the same about adultery, vengefulness, greed, self-righteousness and an unforgiving spirit. This is to say that while homosexual practice is sin, it is not the only sin, but one sin among many which estrange us from God. We follow Jesus as we welcome all sinners to repent, to receive the forgiveness of God and to enter into the fellowship of God's people.

Barbara noted and later told me that she chose these less-condemning statements from among nine listed in the report. It was no wonder that I feared not being welcome in the faith I grew up in. Even the most tolerant leaders of the church considered me a sinner.

❦❦❦❦

I hadn't talked with Janie in a very long time. Despite the anguish our separation brought to my heart, I reminded myself that this was the only life I could ever have in regard to her. I no longer allowed myself to live in the unrealistic fantasy world I'd created.

❦❦❦❦

Barbara and I began discussing the phrase "hate

the sin, love the sinner" after I told her how much I hated that phrase. She replied that she wasn't crazy about it and could easily see how I might hate it. She saw no sin in being born with a specific sexual identity but couldn't find any part of the Bible that condones any sexual relationship other than a faithful heterosexual marriage. That would include premarital sex and adultery, obviously. She said that she imagined few people in any Sunday-school class were free from all sexual sin, but doubted many would be honest about that fact since they didn't have to be.

She also couldn't imagine interrupting a friendship because of any judgment she might make as to sin in someone else's life. This would leave her with zero friends—and no one who'd be willing to be her friend, since her sinful characteristics were painfully obvious to anyone who'd spent much time with her.

I tried to analyze Barbara's opinion about homosexuality and concluded that she accepted the fact that people don't choose to be homosexual but felt quite strongly that relationships between homosexuals were sinful.

❧❧❧❧

I read somewhere that once an individual decided to come out of the closet, it was a never-ending process. That's true. Every once in a while I felt a nudge to tell a certain individual. After I thought about it for a while, I usually decided this was a step I needed to take, and then I'd do it. For the most part, the responses were positive, and I began developing closer friendships with more and more people.

Barbara and I wrote several letters back and forth

one night. Barbara said that she remembered how unclear she was as to who she was as a person when she was in high school and at Baylor University, and she tried to imagine what it must have been like for me in much more difficult circumstances. She had no problem staying aware of the pain I had endured for so many years, never knowing if anyone cared about me for myself or just who they thought I was.

One good thing about pain, it certainly makes a person compassionate—and we all need a certain amount of compassion.

I replied that I'd focused on her statement about never knowing if anyone cared about me for myself and told her she was right. I'd played a role all my life. I'd always tried to be good and follow all the rules. I'd wanted to be accepted, and I'd especially wanted my parents to be proud of me. I'd known they suspected I was homosexual and that they believed homosexuality was wrong and totally unacceptable for their only daughter. I'd walked this tightrope all of my life— pretending to be someone I wasn't in order to please my parents and society in general.

I could never let my guard down with anyone. Even when Karen and I continued to correspond, I was always cautious and circumspect, knowing her husband also read my letters.

The loneliness hurt the most. The challenge of succeeding at whatever I attempted was always just that, a challenge. This constant striving to be best became a way of life. Actually, I was trying to prove my worth more to myself than to anyone else. And I'm still caught up in that. I guess when you do something all your life, it's difficult to change.

My willingness to share my secret amazes me. So many have told me how courageous I am, but I don't feel courageous at all—just free. Unshackled. Out of bondage.

Chapter Twenty-five

I received an e-mail from Frank, a friend who works with Vicki, one of the women I sent my out-of-the-closet letters to months ago but hadn't heard from. Frank wrote that he'd had the most amazing and refreshing conversation with Vicki. He hadn't brought the subject up; Vicki had. Vicki asked Frank if he'd received the e-mail from me about my news. He said that he had and had known for quite some time.

Vicki stated that she still loves me as a friend and would never shun me, but she did disagree with my choice and its effect on Jim. Frank commented that it wasn't a choice but that God had made me that way. Vicki said she just couldn't believe God made homosexuals. She also said she didn't know very much about homosexuality and really couldn't make that judgment. Frank very politely told Vicki that they would have to agree to disagree on the subject and explained to her why he didn't believe it was a choice. Vicki said she was very proud of the comments my pastor made to me and acknowledged that he was a very compassionate man.

Vicki also told Frank that she wanted to respond to my e-mail to let me know that she still cared about me as a friend but wasn't sure what to say. She and her husband had lengthy discussions on the subject, and she indicated she would send a message to me as soon as she collected her thoughts.

*I feel you have a friend in Vicki...I think she's trying
to keep an open mind. It was a very positive conversation.
Good for you, girl!*

Frank's sharing about Vicki both excited me at
the possibility of her acceptance as well as disappointed
me in the sense her acceptance was not immediate,
something she was going to have to think about. (Fifteen
years have now passed, and I've yet to hear from her.)

⚜ ⚜ ⚜ ⚜

I dreamed about Karen. We were visiting the
Smithsonian, although it didn't look at all like the
famous museum I enjoyed visiting. But that's where we
were. I could still see her sitting in a chair facing me.
As I looked at her, I thought that she was really quite
attractive. Her makeup, as usual, was flawless, her blond
hair perfectly styled, and, of course, she was still quite
young. In my mind she would always be nineteen.

The two of us experienced an all-encompassing
feeling of comfortableness with each other. At one point
we became separated when one of us left a restroom
ahead of the other, but in a very short period of time
we were effortlessly drawn together again. I didn't recall
our ever touching each other, yet I felt enveloped by
contentment.

⚜ ⚜ ⚜ ⚜

I was both surprised as well as elated to have a
phone message from Janie. She explained that she'd
been in Austin all this time because her aunt had fallen

and broken her hip.

I'd already convinced myself (how many times had I done this?) that Janie no longer wanted to have anything to do with me. Each time I was always surprised (and relieved) to learn I was wrong.

꧁꧂꧁꧂

Brenda invited me to her home, where nine of us gathered for good food and games such as Scattergories and Trivial Pursuit. It was a good time, and I really enjoyed the evening.

I'd received two written requests from Carolyn to come back and visit our Sunday-school class. As our class's new teacher, she believed I hadn't returned because I felt uncomfortable in the group and was right, in a way. But the feeling of being ill at ease had nothing to do with everyone's knowing I'm gay. It had everything to do with sitting in a room with Janie and being fearful that I'd look, act, or speak to her in some way that would let others know I was in love with her. I didn't want that to happen. And I also didn't want to inflict pain on myself by being in such close proximity to her. I hoped that wouldn't happen but was ready to give it a try—to experiment.

When I headed to church for the early service, I decided to attend Carolyn's class. I felt right at home with this group. Everyone kept asking where Janie was, and no one seemed to know. Then, a week later, as I again took my seat in my old Sunday-school class, Carolyn walked over and sat beside me. "Do you know anything about Janie?" she asked.

"I haven't talked with her for a long time," I admitted, "but I do know that her aunt fell and broke her hip."

Then, in a surprised voice, Carolyn said, "Well, there she is now."

I didn't look. I hadn't seen her in such a long time I wasn't certain how I'd respond. Carolyn then commented, "She's heading our way."

I finally turned around. No pain when I saw her. I was so relieved. I felt no pain at all. She looked as wonderful as always, and we greeted each other as she sat down beside me. Still no pain. When we entered our classroom, I debated the wisdom of sitting beside her but decided that everyone would expect me to, and my not sitting next to her would raise unnecessary questions. So I did what was expected of me, all the time feeling comfortable in her presence. I was excited to realize I could look at her, talk to her, and still feel no pain. Relief flooded through me, along with a hope that the worst was over. I was healing.

I called Janie that afternoon because she'd asked for details about an upcoming appearance by Rabbi Kushner. We talked for a long time. So enjoyable. But again, no pain. I was thrilled and relieved. How wonderful it would be to feel nothing but friendship toward Janie.

❧ ❧ ❧ ❧

Greg, the friend I occasionally chauffeur around, sent me an e-mail explaining that he'd contacted a counselor friend of his about me. Greg still had difficulty understanding my claim to be lesbian. He thought I'd jumped the gun and that I couldn't be a lesbian if I wasn't having an affair with a woman. This had been a very difficult issue for him.

He shared with me the letter his counselor friend had sent to him.

Got your e-mail. Yes, I do know something about lesbians. As with any sexual-orientation issues, this one has more to do with how a person experiences intimacy with other people, and not just sexual intimacy (that's actually the easy part). So the fact that she has not actually had genital sexual contact with another woman would not mean that she is premature in claiming that she is a lesbian. She would know that pretty well before she ever has a girlfriend.

Think back to being a teenager. You were pretty sure whom you wanted long before you found a way to actually score with a woman. Although you had not had any heterosexual genital sexual intimacy, you were quite correct to assume you were heterosexual. In much the same way, the sixty-year-old woman can say that she is a lesbian. Sexual activity is not determinative of sexual orientation. Sexual orientation is determinative of sexual activity. You can have the orientation without ever having the activity.

Sexual orientation is so much more than a preference or a choice. It is not a matter of liking something the way we like (or dislike) cherry Cokes, for instance. It is a whole different way of experiencing the world.

In our world, it is not at all unusual for someone sixty years old to finally get around to recognizing that their true orientation is as a lesbian. Many, many, many lesbians marry and have children (sometimes finding no other options in their world at the time) and eventually recognize and find the courage to act upon their true orientation. It does not invalidate the good times and the good feelings that almost certainly were present in the marriage. It does not mean the marriage was a lie.

I think we are moving into a world that will not FORCE young people to marry. Lesbians will not be forced into heterosexual marriages. Society will not push as hard for conformity. We will celebrate diversity and welcome it even in our own families. (I have a dream...)

We will not be so quick to demonize the adult actions of people different from us. We will decriminalize consenting intimate actions between consenting adults. We will let people love whom they will.

The Church will have to quit loading the rifles of people they are setting up to persecute those whom the church regards as sinners. We will have to learn to let God be God and not get ourselves mixed up on this point and start acting like "vengeance is mine," because the Lord said, "Vengeance is MINE, I will repay." We can get comfortable knowing that, all these years, God has run the Universe without needing me to stick MY nose in and punish sinners. My job is to confess MY sins, not others' sins. Oh, yes, I have a dream today.

And if we can make some of those dreams come true, we will have worked to make our prayer come true ("Thy Kingdom come, on earth... "), at least on our little corner of the earth, and in our hearts.

Tell your friend that you know she did not come to her decision easily, and that you know it took lots of courage to say and do what she did. Tell her that you will be praying that she will find new strength with each day to be the person God created her to be.

Greg, nobody can CHOOSE to become a lesbian. That is a matter of creation. (For that matter, nobody can CHOOSE to be straight; that, too, is a gift of the Creator.)

We are what we are. It is what we CHOOSE to do about it that separates the women from the girls, in the case of this sixty-year-old lesbian.

Of course, when anybody asks me, I tell them don't wait till you're sixty to get real with yourself and your family. Get with it, time's a-wasting! Be who you ARE. Let the chips fall. Let other people figure it out; you are responsible for yourself. Don't be captive of other people's ignorance and prejudice.

Move on. And anyone who refuses to bless you, move away from that person—no one needs their condemnation.

And I rant and rave some more, because I think it is criminal what happens to lesbians and gay men in our society. But sometimes it is with their own consent and cooperation that they are persecuted.

I think your sixty-year-old might merit a medal for valor.

What a letter! I was ecstatic upon reading it and shared it with Barbara, Brenda, and Janie.

Chapter Twenty-six

B renda wrote me on October 11.

Happy Coming Out Day! How does it feel? I think we should celebrate.

I greeted her the same way and told her that I wouldn't trade it for anything.

I was attending another Beth Moore Bible study, and this one had to do with bondage and setting ourselves free. It was a hard study for me, and this past week had been especially difficult. However, the video lesson that day (about sixteen women were there) had focused on one type of bondage handed down from one generation to another—prejudice.

The only prejudice mentioned was racial prejudice, but that certainly wasn't the prejudice I'd had to live with that had impacted my life decisions. I'd used a bunch of tissues but didn't think anyone noticed. Some in the group knew about me, but it was a small minority.

I felt emotionally drained but told Brenda that celebrating was fine with me.

❧❧❧❧

I wrote Brenda the following day about a concert in Bergfeld Park at seven thirty Saturday evening featuring the East Texas Symphony Orchestra. They planned to play Tchaikovsky, Gershwin, Debussy, Grieg, Strauss, Berlioz, and Bizet.

Can't beat that! (Except no Schubert or Mozart). Anyway, are you interested in going? Many of the selections were listed in yesterday's newspaper and they sound wonderful.

Brenda replied that I'd "beaten her to the draw." She'd read about the concert and was thinking along the same lines, saying it sounded like a great lesson in the classics to her. She asked if I wanted to come over to her house and then walk to the park. Or maybe I could come earlier and she could fix something. Or we might split a Bruno's half lasagna or one of their large salads.

As I drove Greg around that day, I mentioned the upcoming concert, indicating my plans to attend.

"Alone?" he asked.

"No, I'll go with a friend."

"A man?"

"Now, Greg, why would I go with a man?"

"Well, what's her name?"

"Brenda."

Then later in the afternoon I told him about a movie I'd seen that I thought he'd enjoy, called *Saving Grace*. Again he put me through the usual quiz as to whether I went alone or with whom. I again had to tell him, "Brenda."

He jumped to all kinds of wrong conclusions, despite my protests to the contrary. He then asked, "Where did you meet her?"

"At a PFLAG meeting." And then I explained the group to him. Greg was a slow learner, but he kept plugging along.

❧❧❧❧

At church one night, while our pastor was leading a discussion in our fellowship hall, Barbara moved her chair so she could sit close to her husband. That display of harmony caused my heart to ache. I actually felt resentment as they enjoyed each other's company and companionship. Their affection for each other was publicly acceptable, whereas Barbara's interpretation of scripture prohibited me from experiencing anything similar.

❧❧❧❧

I was afraid Brenda might become personally interested in me. I didn't want her to be hurt, and I didn't want to lead her on. We'd never touched each other, but our friendship was deepening.

❧❧❧❧

Looking back on the past year of turmoil, I realized God had sent special people into my life to help me over the really rough spots. That past May, an e-mail friend had sent me the following paper titled "People." It had hit home when I read it, so I filed it for future reference. And as I looked at it again, it seemed to be even more apropos to the past year of my life.

People come into your life for a reason, a season, or a lifetime. When you figure out which it is, you know exactly what to do. When someone is in your life for a REASON, it is usually to meet a need you have expressed outwardly or inwardly.

They have come to assist you through a difficulty, to provide you with guidance and support, to aid you physically, emotionally, or spiritually. They may seem like a godsend, and they are. They are there for the reason you need them to be. Then, without any wrongdoing on your part or at any inconvenient time, this person will say or do something to bring the relationship to an end.

Sometimes they die. Sometimes they walk away. Sometimes they act up or out and force you to take a stand. What we must realize is that our need has been met, our desire fulfilled; their work is done. The prayer you sent up has been answered and it is now time to move on. When people come into your life for a SEASON, it is because your turn has come to share, grow, or learn.

They may bring you an experience of peace or make you laugh. They may teach you something you have never done. They usually give you an unbelievable amount of joy. Believe it! It is real! But, only for a season. LIFETIME relationships teach you lifetime lessons; those things you must build upon in order to have a solid emotional foundation.

Your job is to accept the lesson, love the person/ people (any way), and put what you have learned to use in all other relationships and areas of your life. It is said that love is blind but friendship is clairvoyant.

Thank goodness for all the friends who had stood by me.

The thought crossed my mind several times that day (a week before Thanksgiving) that only a year ago I was living in (surviving) misery and despair. How much better off I was now. I occasionally sang to myself as I took my walks. Such a change!

Brenda called to invite me to her house the next afternoon to watch a video and eat soup and cornbread. She'd also invited a male friend who didn't cook for himself. I was looking forward to it. As I watched a TV show that night, a scene of a couple gently kissing for the first time awoke a feeling in me that I thought had disappeared.

I thought about Brenda and the possibility of kissing her.

❧ ❧ ❧ ❧

I'd promised myself to mention some dreams I had that past week. The one I had last night was almost a nightmare. I couldn't recall the exact reason, but in the dream I'd returned to the house to live with Jim. It seemed as if it were against my will, an unwelcome change in my life. A cousin whom I haven't seen in over forty years was in the dream. She was still a beautiful young twenty-year-old, but blind. It seemed as if I'd returned to the house to care for her. I recalled my feelings in dreading the bedtime, worried that I would be expected to sleep again with Jim and not wanting to. Part of me kept saying, "This can't happen to me because I'm divorced now," yet I was so afraid it really was going to happen, and I dreaded it.

Dreams are so strange. Where do they come from?

About three nights ago, Karen's mother and father were in my dream. They didn't look at all like they should, but I knew who they were. In the dream, her dad was a large, handsome, well-built man with light-brown hair who was probably in his late thirties or early forties. In reality he was a short, stooped, bearded intellectual. In the dream he put his arm around me, handed me a check for a thousand dollars, and apologized for the problems he and his wife had caused Karen and me, then apologized for making our lives so miserable by not accepting us as partners. I wanted to tear up the check and throw it at him. But I took it, telling myself it was a pittance compared to the years of suffering caused by our parents' lack of acceptance of Karen's and my love for each other.

Evidently my subconscious had been hard at work all those months processing what I was trying to deal with in my waking moments.

Chapter Twenty-seven

Thanksgiving! A wonderful day. Everything about it turned out practically perfect. I walked that morning, despite the mist and sprinkles.

I accompanied Brenda to the service at St. Dismas, a small open and affirming community, and thoroughly enjoyed the mass and being with the approximately twenty people who gathered for the service. Everyone present had had to combat some problem—death of a child, alcoholism, drug addictions, homosexuality, etc. In other words, we were all broken, mending people coming together to support each other. It felt good being there. The pot-luck meal was absolutely delicious.

Afterward, Brenda and I went to my apartment to watch *Angela's Ashes*. As usual, we sat on the floor with our backs against the sofa. A large vicuna rug provided a soft seat for us, and pillows at our backs made this a comfortable viewing position.

After the movie, we saw the last part of *Who Wants to Be a Millionaire*, then the beginning of some news show. As we watched the TV together, our hands occasionally touched, and then we'd pull away. Neither one of us wanted to be the one to make the first move to hold hands, yet apparently we both wanted the same thing. Finally, Brenda took my hand. "Do you mind?"

"No, not at all."

A little later Brenda suggested we turn off the TV and just talk, which suited me fine. At one point, I turned toward her and said, "I realize the Prozac hasn't completely taken away all my feelings."

At this comment she gently kissed me. My response was so positive that we were quickly in each other's arms.

I could never describe the wonderful feeling—as if I'd come home to what I'd always wanted—to hold and kiss a woman. It was absolutely fantastic. I kept thinking, it's been over forty years since I've felt like this, forty years since I've held and kissed a woman.

Kissing Brenda was so natural for me, so desirable. I'd thought the Prozac had numbed all my sexual feelings, but I discovered that night that this wasn't true. Despite our passionate feelings, we both held back. I had a lot of thinking to do on that subject. She felt wonderful. At one point she called me "sweet," and my heart pounded. She was worried about me, afraid I was being overwhelmed with guilt, and asked during one of our cooling-off periods, "Are you crying?"

I assured her I was all right. I wasn't crying. I kept telling her how good she felt to me.

What worried me the most about all of this was that I still had feelings for Janie. The pain still came when I allowed myself to think about her. I felt like I was being very unfair to Brenda to be kissing her when I knew I wasn't completely over my infatuation with Janie. But it wasn't as if I was deceiving Brenda. She knew about Janie. I just didn't want to ever hurt Brenda. I didn't want to use her. And this worried me.

❧❧❧❧

I left for Austin the next morning. Since Mother had broken her hip in August, I'd been caring for her every day, many times around the clock. Now that she was able to get up and around on her own, I felt a need to get away for a while. Laura was visiting a friend in New York City and had invited me to stay in her apartment, so I accepted her offer and enjoyed a few days of freedom from all responsibilities.

I thought about Brenda a lot, wishing she were there with me. I often considered calling her but had no idea what I would say except that I was missing her. I've always felt more comfortable talking with someone in person than over the phone.

After spending the weekend in Austin, I picked up Laura at the airport at noon, took her back to her apartment, then drove directly from Austin to Tyler (224 miles) in order to be at handbell practice by five thirty and was only five minutes late. It was good to be home.

The morning after I returned to Tyler, Janie called. I couldn't believe it but was absolutely delighted. She said it had been at least three weeks since we'd seen each other, and we chatted for an hour and a half. She wanted to know what was going on in my life, so I told her about kissing Brenda.

"What was it like?" she asked.

"Wonderful."

"Oh, I'm SO glad!"

And I knew she was. She'd been wanting me to find someone for such a long time. She asked me if Brenda liked me.

"I think so."

"Well, she'd have to be nuts not to be absolutely crazy about you."

"Oh, Janie!"

"No, that's right. You're such a precious person."

We then discussed some problems she was experiencing. My heart ached for her. She was grieving so deeply and had been for a long time.

That night I sent Brenda an e-mail telling her I was home and inviting her to come over for supper. Five days had passed since we last saw each other and kissed for the first time. I'd had an e-mail the next morning saying she'd just received the invitation and wanted to know which night I meant.

"Tonight," I said, explaining it would be a simple meal. Later, Brenda told me she was so delighted that I wanted to see her again, she shouted in joy.

I prepared a quiche and pistachio ambrosia salad. After the meal, we enjoyed hugging and kissing. My feelings for Brenda were growing daily, which pleased me very much.

She came the next night to use my computer, and we again ended up being affectionate. I couldn't believe all this was happening to me. I was so happy and felt absolutely no guilt, no shame.

A long letter from Brenda arrived, a letter she wrote after she returned home that night.

Dear Lou Anne,

I came home, put myself in a tub of hot water, bathed in candlelight, and soothed by the music of Yanni, I began to weep. Yanni's melodies are so passionate and soulful they often pluck chords of emotion in me.

When I first met you, I felt some interest/attraction. I saw you not only as courageous, but also as someone who had some common experiences, someone who could be a friend, someone who was single and could be a partner in just doing things. And I confess to a bit of physical attraction. I've always thought you were/are cute as a bug.

As we visited and I got to see you more, I liked what I saw. You're an amazing woman—courageous, caring, desiring truth, determined to live in truth, and having the fortitude to keep moving, growing, and being who you are and becoming. I also admire your sensitivity, humor, intelligence, and playfulness.

I just wanted to be available for friendship, encouragement, and support for you—even knowing at the same time my own need for friendship, encouragement, and support. Yes, just a friend as you dealt with your full plate—leaving your marriage, coming out, your struggles and disappointments with church and friends, your getting through your feelings about Janie, and then your mother's illness. And I thought I was pretty successful in cutting off any physical/romantic attractions I might have had. Had a lot of practice in that, you know.

These last few weeks as we've spent more time together, conversing and sharing, I've had to be honest with myself about my growing attraction—my desire to hold you, touch you gently, and kiss you passionately. I couldn't stay away from you and let the feelings die a painful natural death over time, nor could I be around you and continue to ache inside.

So Thanksgiving evening—oh, I want you to know I was so proud and pleased to have you with me at St. Dismas—I mustered every ounce of courage I might have and said, "Let's turn the TV off and talk." I held your hand, and when you turned to me and said that the Prozac hadn't killed everything, that you were feeling something, I kissed you.

I admit I was a bit surprised but very pleased with your response—warm and tender—as if you might like me.

I don't know about you, Lou Anne, but I'm definitely in uncharted territory here. I feel happy and excited, as well as a little (a lot) of uncertainty. I was thinking as I wept earlier in the bathtub—What do I want? This is my answer.

I want you and me to listen to Yanni's music together. I want you to hear the song "Desperado," and then you'll know my greatest fear and pain. I want to dance with you while Kenny Gee plays.

Yes, I want to dance with you literally. I also want us to keep dancing—figuratively, as well. I want to keep doing the steps as whatever it is—be it friendship or relationship—between us develops into whatever it's supposed to be. I don't have a clue. I just know I'm tired of running from myself and others. I want to do it differently this time.

Well, Lou Anne, I hope some of this makes a little sense. I just want to be honest. I've said a lot about me and what I want—aren't I self-centered? I'll close with as much honesty and lack of self-centeredness as I can muster by saying I love you. I truly want for you what is best and good for you in your life.

I love you,
Brenda

What a thrill! I was flattered that she liked me enough to write a long letter—and to be so open and honest about her feelings.

I replied by saying that I didn't intend to comment much over the Internet about the wonderful letter I'd just received and that I was counting the hours until I saw her.

Brenda immediately invited me to eat spaghetti with her that night, then afterward to help her decorate her Christmas tree. She began at that time to hold and kiss me the minute one of us stepped inside the other's dwelling. We just held and kissed.

Supper was delicious, and it was nice being with her. I was learning to appreciate her more and more. Intelligent, kind, giving, respected, cute, and most honorable and truthful, she's one in a million. I'm very fortunate that she cares for me so much.

Putting lights on her tree didn't take long, so we had hours to enjoy holding and kissing. Despite the Prozac's dulling of my emotions, I experienced a passion I hadn't felt in more than forty years. I found it unbelievable that I was now finding life so enjoyable and that I looked forward to the next day, the next week, the next year. Unbelievable!

When I awoke Sunday morning, I wished Brenda were there with me. Not Janie, but Brenda! Now that was a welcome change.

❧❧❧❧❧

I was already seated in Sunday school when Janie walked across the room to sit beside me. Seeing her brought no sensation of longing, no pain. A calmness permeated me, and I realized my intense feelings toward her had vanished. What a relief!

❧❧❧❧❧

I didn't call Brenda. Many times I wanted to, but I just didn't. I had no idea why. I just didn't. At both the morning and evening church services, I wished she were sitting beside me. But if she had been there, it would have been very difficult not to hold her hand, and

I didn't think my church was ready for that. But even late that Sunday night, I was thinking of her, wishing she were here.

⁂

Prior to the evening church service, Laura had called. The subject turned to politics, and she said she really was ready to get this disputed election between Bush and Gore over. She was in the minority at her office. Her boss, a Baptist, had said to her the other day, "We Christians *know* Bush is the better man."

"I'm not going to tell you what I said back to him," she told me.

"Go ahead and tell me."

"I said, 'Bullshit!' Don't include ME in your WE comment as if all Christians are Republican!"

Her boss had then apologized to her for making the comment.

I e-mailed Brenda, telling her of the incident and added, "Don't ask me where she got her nerve."

Brenda replied, "Oh, I *know* where she got her nerve. I look forward to meeting Laura." After writing a little about one of her sons, she added, "I can't find any words to describe Saturday."

Chapter Twenty-eight

I called my doctor to ask when I could get off the Prozac. Because I had practically no emotions, I didn't want to stay on it much longer.

Friday, December 8 was marvelous, as Brenda spent the night with me. Feeling a woman's body next to mine for the first time in over forty years was heavenly, as if I was where I was supposed to be. I felt calm, happy, and contented, with no feelings of guilt or shame. I visualized Jesus standing beside the bed, smiling down upon us with the most glorious, approving smile.

The feeling of His blessed Presence delighting in our happiness was more meaningful to me than any marriage ceremony. During my thirty-seven years of marriage to a man, I never pictured Jesus being anywhere near our marriage bed or in any way approving of our physical relationship. Yet I was now feeling His approval throughout my whole being. I knew that in God's eyes Brenda and I had married each other. My happiness was so overwhelming I seemed to be constantly reminding myself it was real—that holding Brenda in my arms was no dream. I savored every minute, aware that I was feeling a physical closeness I'd spent many years longing for.

Saturday night we attended an all-lesbian party, which was a first for me. Invitations went out to 117 lesbians, and at least eighty people were there. (To think I knew no lesbians a year ago!) We ate lots of fantastic food, were entertained by an all-girls band, and played some crazy games that had me in stitches as I realized I'd led a very sheltered life.

❧❧❧❧❧

I mailed about eighty Christmas letters that year, which announced—in addition to news of my divorce, my church activities, the birth of a new grandson, and my mother's broken hip—that I was much happier than I'd been in a long, long time. Tears sprang to my eyes as I concluded the letter like this.

I recently read the following: "By the grace of God, our suffering can be transformed into something that brings life and light to this world." I believe that is what is happening in my life, and I praise the Lord for his tender care and guidance.

May knowing that you are in the hands of an all-powerful, all-loving God bring you peace.

Lou Anne

❧❧❧❧❧

Cold, cold weather. It was beautiful outside with all the ice, but tree limbs were breaking off, power was out in many parts of town, traffic signals didn't all work, and water pressure was going down. This turned out to be a terrible ice storm. Some homes were without electricity for a month or more.

I was quite surprised to receive a letter from a fellow in Dallas that Jim and I had known in the early sixties. Actually, he'd been a friend of Jim's prior to our marriage, and we'd occasionally visited in his home.

He'd received my Christmas card (with letter) and replied that he appreciated receiving my card and had thought of me frequently this year.

I had a note from Jim via e-mail. He and I go a long ways back, and he shared the info about the divorce. Bless his heart, he's still hurting from it, but I fully understand and appreciate YOUR feelings, too. I probably understand your vantage point more than I do his. As I explained to Jim, I've known that I'm gay for many years now. I had to reconcile that fact with my wife and our son quite a while ago. I enjoyed your quote about transforming our suffering into something bringing life and light into the world. Very true, indeed. My wife remarked over and over again about how the Holy Spirit marches through our lives wearing combat boots. Also a very apt expression. I still have a few cleat marks to show for that presence.

I hope we can stay in touch and that your life is proceeding happily in the direction you want it to take. I wish for you only the best. Know that our friendship remains solidly intact.

Best always...

I immediately responded, telling him how much I appreciated his note and his understanding.

It's as if we are all members of the same club—put on earth to support each other. I've been amazed at how many of my friends are affected by either being gay or having a gay child. If everyone came out of the closet at once, the nation would be flabbergasted.

I then told him my story as to why I married and

what my life had been like. I concluded by thanking him for his honesty and telling him I was glad he had a partner, that my recent involvement with a woman had brought me a peace and contentment I hadn't felt for a long time.

He answered right away and shared his story with me, saying that his wife had had a tough time at first but later became his staunchest advocate.

She'd remark, "Honey, you didn't ask to be gay any more than I asked to have MS." Very tolerant, very understanding. I was blessed to have that sweet thing in my life those thirty years—even if I WAS hiding the truth from her and me both.

He also admitted that when he came out to Jim not long ago, he'd obviously hit him too close to home, because he'd never received a reply to his letter.

When I shared with Barbara the letter I'd written to my Dallas friend, she found it interesting that I'd recently become involved with a woman, though she'd suspected it. She said she supposed I meant Brenda and she hoped to get to know her better.

She also warned me to take it slow and easy in any new relationship and to be very sure before I committed to someone else.

When I'd answered Barbara later that day, I admitted I'd decided to let the cat out of the bag because I figured she knew anyway. I reminded her that Brenda and I had met on April 10 and didn't hold hands until Thanksgiving.

Then I said that Brenda and I had every intention of growing old together and that, since I wasn't far from the "old" category, we laughingly talked about the future when she will use a walker to push my wheelchair.

৶৶৶৶

Janie and I ate together at McAllister's and visited about an hour and a half. Afterward, I wrote Brenda about the meeting to tell her how delighted I was to realize my painful feelings toward Janie had disappeared. Hallelujah!

What a blessed relief to be able to sit and visit with Janie and not experience that old yearning for something I could never have. Janie was also delighted.

I shared the good news not only with Brenda, but also with Barbara, who quickly replied.

Now THERE'S a Christmas gift! How are you doing without Prozac? How are preparations coming for your mother's ninetieth birthday party? In other words, are you doing okay? Is life becoming more joyful for you more of the time? Can you sit down and read a book?

Your nosy but caring friend,
Barbara

I replied that this Christmas, compared to last year's, would be much different for me.

It's as if I have to pinch myself constantly to be assured my feelings of happiness and contentment are real. I've just completed my two-week withdrawal period for the Prozac and took my last pill yesterday morning. This week, and possibly the next, will tell the tale.

৶৶৶৶

I wrote a coming-out letter to Marta, a friend from the sixties. Her reply pleased me and brought back memories.

She said she wasn't shocked but hadn't realized how unhappy I'd been.

In the 1966-68 scheme of things, I saw only a dedicated, wonderful, beautiful wife and mother, somewhat reserved but always giving unstintingly of herself. You were the pie-crust wizard who showed me that working in the least amount of water equaled flakier; you shared recipes I still have; and you and Jim were always available for forays to the Night Hawk or such for food and fun. You were the one with a burning desire to write. You were the one who stretched herself to meet a most interesting variety of jobs over the years. Your Christmas letters always brought news of some additional mastery...always humble, always capable and skilled.

I admired you enormously then, and I admire and respect you enormously now. Your letter gives me a broader perspective, and I understand that only your courageous stand could relieve a pervasive pain of forty years' endurance. I applaud you and am thankful for the support of your children. Forty years in the wilderness. May you surely know the presence of the Lord as He holds you in the palm of His hand.

It seems the older I get, the more flimsy and useless our facades are and the only true dialogue is soul to soul. I sense that is what you have shared with me here, and I am deeply touched.

Love, Marta

Our letters reminded me that my parents never spoke openly about my homosexuality. However, one afternoon after I'd been married almost twenty years and already had my fourth child, my dad had privately said to me, "I want to apologize for what I once thought about you." His statement came completely out of the blue, but I knew exactly what was on his mind although this was a subject he and I had *never* broached. Actually Mother had brought up the subject only the one time when I was seventeen. My being homosexual was like the proverbial elephant in the living room.

I didn't ask Dad, "To what are you referring?" I *knew* to what he referred.

At that time, I could have simply accepted his apology and thereby let him believe he'd made a terrible mistake when he convinced Mother I was a homosexual, or I could confess that he owed me no apology because he'd been correct—I am homosexual.

Confessing to the truth, however, would deeply hurt him, hurt him more than having judged me unfairly. At least that's what I'd concluded.

I therefore replied, "That's all right, Dad. No problem." And that's all that was ever said between us on this subject. Dad passed away in 1996 at age eighty-six, and I lost my chance to tell him I'm a lesbian. I wonder what he would have said.

Chapter Twenty-nine

The contentment Brenda and I felt was based upon the assurance that in God's sight we were as married as any heterosexual couple. We knew this to be true because when we were together, we were enveloped in a sense of peace and serenity, invariably aware of Christ's presence as well as of His fantastic gift in bringing us together.

I once heard because we were taught that homosexuals are bad people, and because we don't see ourselves as bad people, we therefore have to conclude that we must not be homosexual. But Brenda and I had finally acknowledged that we really are homosexual. In accepting this fact, we'd braced ourselves to be overwhelmed with guilt, with a feeling that we must be bad. When this feeling never materialized, another terribly heavy burden was lifted from our shoulders.

Many nights as we lay in each other's arms, Brenda would sing to me. She has a beautiful voice, and I felt proud whenever she joined me at church and eventually become a member of First Baptist.

One of my church friends asked me in 2001, "Who's that cute girl who sits with you in church?" At first her question baffled me, but then I realized she'd been viewing Brenda and me from the choir loft. I proudly shared with her Brenda's name and explained that she was my friend.

❧❧❧❧

In March 2001, Brenda and I attended the Southern Regional PFLAG Conference in Dallas, which gave us an opportunity to be seen in public as a couple. When we registered at the hotel and asked for a room with one bed, I felt self-conscious and nervous, concerned about others' possible negative opinions. But no more hiding, no more pretending, no more doing what was expected by getting a room with two beds and using only one of them. Once we'd crossed that threshold, I found it much easier to ask for one bed the next time, and the next.

As we walked across campus to attend the conference, we often held hands. We'd never held hands publicly in Tyler and enjoyed this opportunity/freedom to exhibit that we were together. It felt so good, so free, so right.

I discovered during the conference's meetings that my emotions were constantly bubbling near the surface. I kept hearing statements I'd never heard before, some I'd never really thought about, yet they applied directly to me. For example, in discussing gender, a speaker pointed out that a person's gender identification has nothing to do with sexual orientation. In other words, in my case, it's all right to be feminine (which I consider myself to be) yet to have a sexual orientation making me desire a woman for a partner. Another way to put it: A woman doesn't have to look or act butch to be a lesbian.

Other comments that hit home included these three: The more painful the outing, the more potential for happiness. When you first hear something affirming about homosexuality, you decide to come out. Negative comments about homosexuality from family cause an individual to stay in the closet. All of these statements were true for me.

As the months passed, I become bolder. My mother passed away in November 2001 at age ninety. Perhaps her death led me to be more visible as a lesbian. Although she and I never had another conversation about my being gay other than the one when I was seventeen, I believe she had been doing some deep thinking about the issue. She obviously realized I'd been very unhappy in my marriage; and by the time of her death, Brenda had become a regular part of my life. My mother was an intelligent woman.

In the summer of 2002, I joined Soulforce in its silent vigil at the Southern Baptist Convention in St. Louis. Soulforce, founded by Mel White, the author of *Stranger at the Gate*, offers a spirit-based activism aimed at reconciliation with those who oppress the gay community. Participating in this vigil, I stood on a sidewalk along with many others, wore a shirt that said STOP SPIRITUAL VIOLENCE, and held a sign that said the same.

Churches preaching the sinfulness of homosexuality and warning that homosexuals are going to hell are committing spiritual violence against gays, lesbians, transgendered, and bisexual individuals. Soulforce fights this type of religion-based oppression, and their message is dear to my heart.

In addition to working with Soulforce, Brenda and I, as an openly gay couple, began working closely with a group of leaders inside the Cooperative Baptist Fellowship. Until the formation of this large umbrella organization, Baptist churches joined the Southern Baptist Convention. But many Baptist churches found they simply could not support the SBC's radically conservative policies. The Cooperative Baptist

Fellowship was formed to offer Baptist churches a more moderate alternative.

Brenda and I, as a gay couple, joined a few gay allies in dialogues with CBF leaders on the subject of homosexuality and the possibility of Baptist churches becoming more open and accepting (or perhaps I should say less condemning and rejecting).

❧❧❧❧

As Janie and I were visiting in July 2002, reviewing all the changes that had taken place in my life, she said, "If it weren't for me, you wouldn't have ruined your life."

I assured her that what she said was ridiculous, but I knew she had assumed a burden of guilt regarding my divorce. Wanting to allay those feelings, I sat down the following day and wrote her.

Janie, I keep thinking about your regret that you had in some way upset my life. You're right. If it hadn't been for you, I'd still be married. But I wouldn't trade my life now for what I had then for all the money, power, and fame the world might offer. No way.

Yes, you changed my life. You changed it by your words of love and acceptance of homosexuals. Your words amazed me. Never in all my life had the thought even occurred to me that a gay person could be loved and accepted.

I truly believe God sent you into my life to set my feet onto this new pathway of activism for homosexuals. I won't downplay the pain I suffered for at least a year, but even so, I can now look back on those events and those emotions and see God's hand at work.

Each time I share my story and each time I have an opportunity to speak up for the LGBT community, I think, if it weren't for Janie, for her kind, loving, and sensitive heart, I wouldn't be here. She's behind every bit of success I experience. One of these days I hope she'll be aware of the part she's played in my demonstrating with Soulforce at the SBC convention, in the letters I've written to the Baptist Standard, *in my meeting with some of the leaders of the Cooperative Baptist Fellowship, and in whatever else I do in this regard.*

Janie, my life now is unbelievably good. I never envisioned I could be happy like I am now. Brenda is truly a gift from God. I'm continually thankful for her, for her love, and for our relationship. But even more than this, I'm free of the fear I lived with all of my life—a fear that someone would discover my shameful secret. I can't explain to someone who hasn't lived with that burden of fear how liberating it is to be unshackled from that bondage. It's absolutely wonderful.

And surely you know I wasn't happy in my marriage. Why should you have any kind of regret that I'm now divorced?

So promise me to never again feel that you're somehow to blame for ruining my life. That's absolutely ridiculous.

Much love, Lou Anne

Less than two hours later, she replied, thanking me for my letter and our friendship.

Believe me, if you think I saved your life, you have no idea how many times you have saved mine. You will make a difference in this world.

I pray every day that she's right.

❧ ❧ ❧ ❧

For about three years, my relationship with Brenda blossomed while I continued to live in my small apartment and she remained in her small home. She was working regular hours, and although I'd retired as a teacher, I became quite active in running the office of a newly formed group developing a faith-based health clinic for the underserved, working poor of our community. My work became quite challenging and time consuming, so Brenda and I became primarily weekend lovers/companions.

We occasionally talked about purchasing a home together and even shared these thoughts with Sidney, a realtor friend who took time to show us some houses. None interested us, but he was forming an idea of what kind of house we wanted. One weekend at the end of August 2003, Sidney called us. "You've got to come see this house. I think it's just what you're looking for, and the price has just been lowered."

"We'll give it some thought, Sidney. Maybe we can find time in a day or two to come see it."

"It's bound to go quickly at this price. You really need to come on over right away."

We again thanked him and hung up. We did think a few minutes about it and decided it might be wise to follow his advice. We called him and told him that we'd meet him there, that we were on our way.

We knew almost immediately that the house was just right for us. The inside was all white, which appealed to me, as I like light. It appealed to Brenda because she has vision problems. When we looked out the sliding-glass back door onto a large wooden deck and saw a lush, green, well-manicured backyard, that pretty well cinched it. This brick, three-bedroom, two-bath home priced at less than $100,000 spoke loudly to our pocketbooks. Other families were also looking at the house while we were there, and Sidney kept urging us to get our bid in before they did. So in less than an hour we were signing papers to purchase our new home.

I mention the house for several reasons, in addition to it being an outward symbol of our committed relationship. Convincing the mortgage company to place both our names on the deed became challenging. It wasn't that they didn't want to be accommodating, but they'd never before had such a request. They didn't seem to know how to do it. But it was done.

In the years to come, we kept reminding them that when they sent us an interest statement at the end of each year, both our names needed to be on the statement—both names in full. I believe one time they had "Lou Anne McWilliams" listed instead of Lou Anne Smoot and Brenda McWilliams. We would just laugh, give them a call, patiently explain what we needed, and they'd do their best to comply. We must have been the only gay couple for whom they'd ever provided a home mortgage.

I wanted to mention this home purchase because we realized after the fact that our moving-in date, October 11, 2003, was national Coming Out Day. We thought that coincidence so appropriate, even though it was accidental. As I write these words toward the end of 2015, we've been in our home for twelve years, leaving us only three more years of mortgage payments. Hooray!

Chapter Thirty

When I began coming out in my church in 2000, I started feeling very uncomfortable. Several members whom I considered friends simply couldn't look me in the eye. That made me feel as if they considered me the very epitome of evil, upon which they could not look. Because of my discomfort, I seriously considered leaving the church and looking for somewhere else to worship.

But God seemed to remind me that I'd been a member of First Baptist for almost twelve years by then and was known as a Christian wife, mother, Sunday-school teacher, handbell ringer, and a very active and supportive member of the congregation. If I left the church, I'd be throwing away all that good will, so to speak. Whereas if I remained, I had an opportunity to be an example of a gay Christian, which to many, if not most (maybe even all the members), was an oxymoron. So despite the discomfort of remaining, that's what I decided to do.

Then when Brenda joined me as a member of First Baptist, together we served as an example of a gay Christian couple in a committed, covenant relationship. We made a point of sitting together in about the third row from the front, close to the center aisle, where each person could see us.

Everyone was nice to us and never mentioned the fact that we were gay. Obviously no one wanted to talk about the subject. The members became accustomed to seeing the two of us together. When only one of us showed up for an event, someone invariably asked where the other was.

Brenda and I were members of different Sunday-school classes and departments. So when one class had a social, we both attended. The only time this became awkward was at a Christmas party my department gave in which a game was played pitting husbands against wives. They didn't know what to do with the two of us, so we were designated judges.

❧❧❧❧

In order to help members know one another better, our church organized Shake and Bake groups. These groups consisted of four to five families of varying ages. Baptist Sunday-school classes are organized according to age, so in a large church like ours, we have few opportunities to know members not in our age bracket.

Each group met once a month for a meal, either in a member's home or in a restaurant. Brenda and I participated in one of the groups in 2002, thoroughly enjoying it. The members we met and visited with became good friends.

Consequently, when new groups were again formed two years later, we signed up to participate. Just prior to the organization of the groups, I listened to a phone message left on my answering machine by Wilson Rhodes, the associate pastor. He explained that the rules had changed with the Shake and Bake groups and that non-married couples would be placed in separate groups.

This new rule, in our opinion, was designed to separate Brenda and me and to prohibit our participation as a couple. I wrote to him expressing my sadness and disappointment with the decision and asked if an engaged heterosexual couple wanted to participate in a Shake and Bake group as a couple, would they be allowed to do so or would they be separated because they were technically still single.

I then started preaching that mainstream churches were regularly driving away people who are different with rules such as this, set up to exclude rather than accept.

Isn't it sad that churches make certain Christians feel unwelcome and/or uncomfortable?

He never replied to my letter.

❧❧❧❧

One of my favorite church stories involves a visiting Bible professor from a nearby Baptist college. In years past, he had served as an interim pastor at First Baptist, and I thought he was wonderful because he thought outside the box. Baptists, in my experience, didn't tend to do that. He was funny, energetic, interesting, and knowledgeable. So when I heard he would be leading a series of Bible studies at our church during the summer of 2005, I told Brenda I wanted to go.

We arrived early enough to sit at the front table, close to the stage where he would be standing and speaking. I was enjoying the study, looking up passages in the scriptures and taking notes. Then he read aloud Matthew 9:10-11: *While Jesus was having dinner at*

Matthew's house, many tax collectors and sinners came and ate with him and his disciples. When the Pharisees saw this, they asked his disciples, "Why does your teacher eat with tax collectors and sinners?"

In an effort to expound on this passage and develop its relevance to our Bible Study group, he stated, "In today's world, Jesus's eating with sinners would be like his eating with ..." He began to grope for a suitable comparison, trying to wrap his thoughts around a modern-day sinner. Eventually, he confidently declared, "It would be like Jesus today eating in the home of lesbians."

I could feel my face glowing red and wished the floor would open and swallow me. People were sitting behind us who were well aware Brenda and I were a couple. I didn't hear anything else he said, concentrating solely on breathing and keeping my cool. When the study ended and we walked out of the room, Brenda said, "He kinda got to you, didn't he?"

"Yes, he did. And I'm going to write him a letter. But I want to think about it for a few days."

And that's what I did, just thought about it. Then I wrote to him, telling him how much I'd always enjoyed hearing him speak and how I had looked forward to his Bible studies. Then I stated that I was sure he had absolutely no idea he had a lesbian couple sitting right in front of him at the Bible study on Wednesday.

Just so you'll know what it's like to eat in the home of lesbians, we would like to invite you and your wife to eat with us Friday evening.

He responded immediately, most apologetic. His faux pas had obviously embarrassed him no end. After thanking us for our dinner invitation, he regrettably declined by explaining that his wife was ill. And we had heard she was on chemo. But he promised to come by for a visit after the next Bible study.

True to his word, he followed us to our home after the next session and visited with us for about an hour. He listened respectfully to Brenda's and my stories. By the time he left, I was convinced it had simply never occurred to this good, kind, highly educated Bible scholar that a Christian could be gay or a gay could be Christian. Hopefully we opened his eyes.

∿∿๛๛

Not long after Brenda joined the church, she quickly became active in the singles department, agreeing to teach a Sunday-school class, becoming the leader of the singles council, and even volunteering to answer the phones during the televised Sunday-morning worship service. As a trained pastoral counselor, she was the ideal person to listen and pray with those who called the church wanting to talk about their problems.

I mention Brenda's commitments to First Baptist as this situation was about to change. In November of 2005, the state of Texas was set to vote on a constitutional amendment called Proposition 2, which stated that a marriage is solely between a man and a woman. Brenda produced a flyer to distribute to our neighbors asking them to vote against this proposition. A picture of the two of us appeared at the top of her well-written letter urging people to reject this attempt to turn our state constitution into a discriminatory document. We distributed copies of the flyer throughout our neighborhood, hanging it on doorknobs. (And yes, this wasn't easy for us to declare in both written and picture form our relationship for all to see. But we more or less gritted our teeth and did it because we felt it was the right thing to do.) When the vote on Proposition 2 was tallied, it passed overwhelmingly, not only in Texas but by well over 90% in our very conservative Smith County.

Very soon after our first political effort as a couple, our church's minister of ministries and missions, Evelyn Carpenter, contacted Brenda, setting up a meeting during the next Wednesday-evening church supper. Because Evelyn gave Brenda no purpose for the meeting, she assumed it must have something to do with the singles department because Evelyn served as the singles director.

Much to Brenda's shock and surprise, Evelyn told her that night that First Baptist had decided she could no longer hold any position of leadership in the church. As Evelyn shared this crushing information, she held a copy of the mustard-colored flyer we had distributed. Someone had obviously taken the flyer to the church, complaining, we supposed, about our membership in the church and the inappropriateness of a gay person being a Sunday-school teacher. Evelyn made it clear to Brenda that she was simply the bearer of the news. She'd been chosen for this unpleasant task because the other church leaders knew she and Brenda were long-time friends and hoped the decision would perhaps appear less harsh coming from her.

Brenda no longer taught her Sunday-school class, no longer led the singles council, and was never again asked to volunteer as a phone counselor during the televised morning-worship service.

This decision by our church was cruel and made me angry. I suppose most people would have walked away from a church that treated them in such a hurtful manner, but we never considered it. We continued volunteering in ways that had nothing to do with leadership positions. And when either of our respective Sunday-school classes needed a substitute teacher, Brenda and I were the ones called upon for that job. We continued to try to serve as a Christian example of a lesbian couple.

≈≈≈≈≈

Barbara battled cancer over the years and seemed to have won the battle. But it returned during 2005 and 2006, when she suffered greatly. Her husband, Jack, cared for her in a wonderful way, and I became a regular visitor. Because Jack loved my chocolate cake, I often baked one for him prior to visiting. When Barbara passed away on July 2, 2006, I lost a wonderful friend. I'll always believe she literally saved my life by standing by me, encouraging me, praying for me, and staying in almost constant contact with me at a time when my despondency was overwhelming me.

I treasure a statement she made after Brenda and I had been together for years. She told me one day, "I'm glad Brenda is part of your life."

I was amazed she said it because she had always held the position that gays should practice celibacy.

≈≈≈≈≈

One Sunday at the end of September 2007, an announcement was made from the pulpit that the church would be sponsoring a Family Campout on November 9 and 10 at our local state park. Brenda and I enjoyed camping, so as soon as the announcement was made, we nudged each other and said, "Let's go!"

When morning worship ended, we headed for the church lobby and picked up an application form. In the next day or two, we completed the form, enclosed our check, and mailed it to the church more than a month prior to the event. Then we marked our calendar.

A month later, two days prior to the campout, I received a phone call from Wilson Rhodes, asking if he could come visit.

"Sure," I replied. He'd never been to our home, so I knew something was up.

When I greeted him at the door and invited him in, he stated, "I guess you know why I'm here."

"Well, it either has to do with your hearing I taught our Sunday-school class last Sunday or with the Family Campout."

"We'll talk about the teaching another time. I'm here about the Family Campout. We think it best you not go." He handed me the envelope I'd mailed to the church.

"Has someone complained?"

"No. I don't think anyone knows you planned to attend."

"Then why do you think it best we not participate?"

"We just think it's best."

"But why?"

"We just think it's best."

That's all he would say. We talked a while longer, and I took the opportunity to share part of my story with him, but tears started to come. I handed him a little booklet to read by Walter Wink titled "Homosexuality and The Bible." He seemed anxious to leave, not at all interested in my story, so I gave up talking with him.

Later on that evening, Brenda attended the Wednesday-evening service and asked Wilson that very important question: "Why did you make this decision?"

He explained that he'd had to really struggle with it. This struck a nerve with Brenda as she retorted, *"You've had to struggle!"*

Later, she felt bad about her reaction and e-mailed him, apologizing for not recognizing that he truly had wrestled with the decision.

Brenda heard nothing from him. Several weeks later, as we sat in the sanctuary waiting for the morning service to begin, he came by, thanked her for her letter, and promised to send her a reply. He never did.

I still have that envelope containing our camp-out application and check as a reminder of the cruel way we were treated. I'm not certain anyone else was even aware this occurred, but I knew Wilson had a very difficult time with my being gay as he was one who, in 2000, couldn't look me in the eye.

Years later I mentioned the camping incident to another church member. She was appalled that we weren't allowed to participate but made me feel better when she shared that she and her husband had once taken part in a family campout.

"Lou Anne," she said, "it wasn't much fun. We older members ended up babysitting the kids to give the younger parents time to themselves. You really didn't miss much."

Chapter Thirty-one

In deciding to stay at the church, we knew we would be facing a wall of prejudice and discrimination, which is exactly why we stayed. We understood the prejudice, why church members believed as they did, and why they were convinced the Bible was very clear on this subject. We knew all this because we'd been indoctrinated with the same misinformation as they had. We didn't hold them to blame, but simply wanted to gently encourage a different way to look at homosexuality and homosexuals by being an example outside the box of who they normally thought homosexuals to be.

After Bob Watson left our church in 2009, our interim pastor was the former dean of Truett Seminary at Baylor University. This former dean, whom I'll call Rick Coates, had, in 2003, withdrawn a scholarship from a young seminary student because he was gay. This action of Dr. Coates had infuriated me, and I wrote to him expressing my displeasure at his decision.

He responded by asking me what an unrepentant person would have to do to be disqualified from the ministry and if he'd taken the scholarship away from a prostitute, drug dealer, thief, wife beater, pedophile, pimp, drug addict, or drunk, would I have written.

I therefore knew his opinions of gays before he preached his first sermon in our church. And sure enough, he preached openly against homosexuality and same-sex marriage. Each time he did, I stood up during his sermon and left the church, walking up the center aisle from the front to the back. The first time I did this, as soon as I reached the outside doors, I turned around to see who might have supported my action and followed me out. No one did. That afternoon I kept waiting for the phone to ring, for a church member to call to apologize for my having to hear such prejudice. No phone calls. No one stood up for me, either literally or figuratively.

After walking out two or three times, I decided to no longer attend the worship service as long as Dr. Coates was there. I also stopped all monetary contributions to the church. And I wasn't silent. I sent letters to the church's finance chairman, to the deacon chairman, and to Dr. Coates, explaining that I could not in good conscience financially support his messages encouraging and inciting prejudice against homosexuals.

When our church called our new pastor in 2011, I returned to our worship services and liked what I saw and heard. Two to three weeks after he arrived, I personally met him for the first time on a Wednesday evening. I'd participated in the Wednesday-evening supper and fellowship and was leaving the church carrying a take-out meal. As I headed out toward the street, our new pastor, Kevin, was walking toward the church.

I greeted him, introducing myself and telling him how delighted we were to have him, that he was like a breath of fresh air. Feeling a need to explain why I was carrying the extra dinner, I stated, "I'm taking supper home to my partner, who has a broken ankle."

As soon as I said "partner," I could tell his mind started whirling. He, with a hopeful sound to his voice, asked, "Business partner?"

"No," I replied. "Domestic partner. We're second-class members of this church."

"Oh, surely not!"

"Yes, we are."

Not wanting to continue this conversation on the sidewalk in front of the church building, I excused myself and left.

A little over a year later, in May 2012, I sat down with Kevin in his study and shared my story with him. He listened very attentively, never argued or debated. After I completed it, he asked me, "Do you remember when we first met?"

"Yes, I certainly do!"

"Well, what did you mean when you said you were second-class members of this church?"

"Kevin, we aren't allowed to hold any positions of leadership here."

Not wanting to make him feel uncomfortable (which seems to be a habit of mine), I said, "I know it's because this church is affiliated with the Southern Baptist Convention and that's their rule. I just wish we weren't, but I know that can never be. We have too many members whose children and grandchildren serve as missionaries for the Southern Baptist Convention, so we'll always be a part of it."

Kevin clearly believed homosexuality was sinful, but by the end of our visit, I felt he might be wavering a little. He felt quite strongly that homosexuality required celibacy, even after I pointed out that the Apostle Paul had stated that celibacy was a gift and that it seemed quite unrealistic to expect every homosexual to be given the gift of celibacy.

Kevin and I remained friends and agreed to

disagree on the issue of homosexuality. I occasionally e-mailed him information, and he answered. I felt we had a good relationship even though we were poles apart.

❦❦❦❦

Brenda and I continued to push against the norm. In late September 2012, we arrived at our church to have our photo made for the new church directory. If you're unfamiliar with church directories, the pictures are organized by family groups. By 2012, Brenda and I had been a family unit for almost twelve years and decided the time had come for our church directory to display a photo of the two of us together. We made sequential appointments for that afternoon's photography session. Arriving on time, we signed in, placing our names in one photo slot. The elderly lady in charge made no comment as we did this.

The photographer did as we asked—took our picture together. Then he suggested we have separate pictures made. So we complied. Afterward we chose one of our couple's photos for the church directory. We ordered various copies of that photo, along with copies of individual shots to share with our children. We felt proud of ourselves to have found the courage to appear together in our church directory. This would certainly be a first for our church.

Five months later, I received an e-mail from our pastor saying that he'd missed us this past Sunday at church and asking us to suggest a date when he could meet with us that week, if possible, in regard to the pictorial directory.

I replied quickly.

It's nice to be missed. We were in Little Rock and were actually visiting a small, African-American congregation Sunday. We happen to know (and like very much) their pastor, Rev. Wendell Griffin, who is also a federal judge. He and I served on a PFLAG panel discussing Religion and the LGBT Community along with a Presbyterian minister, a Methodist minister, a Unitarian minister, and a Jewish rabbi. I was the only layperson and the only Baptist. I was given the opportunity to talk about my book, A Christian Coming Out, *which is due to be published in April. It was an exciting weekend.*

Are you wanting to talk with us about the photo we chose to place in the church directory? We have a full week of obligations and can probably handle whatever question you have by e-mail, if that's all right with you.

He wrote back the next day, remarking on how busy we were and informing us that they needed individual photos for the church directory ASAP. He apologized and thanked me.

I told him that this issue wasn't worth fighting for, but that we'd wanted to give it a try since we'd been together as a stable couple for twelve years and that we'd have individual photos to him by the next night.

He wrote back, saying how grateful he was for my response.

I bathed my e-mail in prayer, as I know e-mails can be wonderful and horrible ways of communicating. I appreciate your understanding, especially given your twelve years together.

Peace

While this correspondence was occurring, I was also writing back and forth with Kay Holladay, our regional PFLAG director. She wrote that they were in the final stages of planning a June 2013 regional PFLAG conference and invited me to speak there.

I immediately replied, thanking her and telling her that I'd love to have this opportunity to share my experiences and talk about my book, which should be available by then. I then told her about our recent church experiences concerning our photo in the church's pictorial directory.

When she replied to say she was tickled that I was going to speak, as she felt I would be "a dynamite closure to the conference," she added this comment.

You and Brenda are my heroes that I look for to emulate grace...I hope your pastor learns some lessons from the two of you—and I hope he sees the essence of what Jesus taught us in you and Brenda.

Chapter Thirty-two

In the last week of May 2013, we drove to Asheville, North Carolina, where on June 3 we picked up 500 copies of my book, *A Christian Coming Out*. I then spoke to nine PFLAG groups, including the regional conference in Norman, Oklahoma, before returning home the end of June.

On July 6, my daughter hosted a surprise party for me to celebrate the publication of my book. I was caught totally unaware. The date of the party happened to be the same date as my eldest grandson's thirteenth birthday, and I thought the party was for him. I even baked him a birthday cake.

As I got ready for the party, I didn't particularly dress up, as I assumed only close family members would be present. Brenda took a look at what I was wearing and suggested I might want to wear a more attractive outfit. She seldom made such a suggestion, but I took her at her word and allowed her to choose from several different options. She chose the dressiest of the lot. Though I found this strange, it still didn't occur to me that I was about to attend anything other than my grandson's birthday party.

Earlier in the week, my daughter had called. "Mom," she'd said. "A neighbor of mine is having a party and has asked to borrow your two card tables and eight fold-up chairs. Could you bring them over to my house?"

I gladly took them to her yet still didn't put any of this together. When we arrived at her home that evening, I assumed all the cars were for the "neighbor's party" and thought nothing of it. But when I walked into my daughter's kitchen carrying the birthday cake, and people who had been waiting elsewhere in the house started appearing, I was baffled. I saw friends from the League of Women Voters. What in the world were they doing there? And then I saw my gay friends walk in, representing both East Texas PFLAG and Project TAG (Tyler Area Gays). They didn't even know my League friends. And why would they be here for my grandson's birthday? Then I spotted Carolyn, my Sunday-school teacher, with her husband.

I don't recall ever feeling quite so confused. It made no sense. Someone pointed out a large banner with my name on it—congratulating me on the publication of my book, and I finally realized the party was for me and not for my grandson, although he and his parents had driven for four hours from Houston for the event.

I was amazed at the variety of friends who attended. My daughter's beautiful home was full to overflowing with happy people, congratulating me. Janie, who had moved to Austin a few years earlier, came along with her sister, who also lived in Austin! What a celebration! Many purchased copies of my book that evening. (Janie bought ten copies to give to friends.)

Later I learned that everyone in my Sunday-school class had been invited to the celebration, but only Carolyn and her husband came. Why didn't the other members come? I so wanted my church family to read my book, to know me, to understand me. I wanted it so much that a week later I sent e-mails to numerous members of my church telling them about my book and explaining how they could order it through my website. I'd known these members for many years, some for almost twenty-five. I felt certain that if they just knew about my book they'd want to read it. If they'd written a book about their life experiences, I'd want to read their story, so foolishly I assumed they'd feel the same about me.

No response. None at all. My Sunday-school teacher purchased a copy at the party, which was the only response I'd had from church members by the middle of July. That hurt, yet I felt if they wouldn't buy my book, I'd simply give them a copy. So on July 14, I dropped one off at our church library. Even as I did this, I felt ill at ease placing the book on the desk in front of the librarian. I knew her, and we'd always gotten along well. A younger woman, she'd hosted our Ladies Round Table Book Club in her home multiple times, and I'd previously been called upon to lead various book discussions.

A month and a half later, on August 30, I received an e-mail from my pastor remarking that we hadn't seen each other recently except from afar and hoping that I had a good summer. Then he explained the situation with my book.

Our librarian let me know that you brought your book by to be available in our library. She has read it in its entirety, and I am reading through it now, as I did not do so when you gave me your manuscript.

While I appreciate the incredible amount of pain you have gone through in your pilgrimage with homosexuality, I do not believe your book to be what we should have in our library on the subject. You and I have already had our discussion about our biblical views of practicing homosexuality and have agreed to disagree on what the Word of God says. I cannot, in good conscience, place a book in the library advocating the practice of homosexuality, even monogamous, as blessed by God, especially as we have people of all ages and levels of Christian maturity utilizing our library.

I do believe aspects of your book could help a mature believer better understand what homosexuals, you and Brenda in particular, have gone through, and how you have reached your conclusion. However, it is not a conclusion that I agree with, nor do not feel it represents our church's convictions.

I am reading another book entitled Washed and Waiting: Reflections on Faithfulness and Homosexuality, *by Wesley Hill, a homosexual and theologian, and am considering making this book available in our library. It is raw, like yours, but ultimately the author concludes that while God can certainly bless him as a homosexual, he must glorify God by practicing celibacy. He believes that the Bible teaches that, in order to be right with God, homosexuals are to remain celibate.*

I do not know whether you have checked to see if your book is available, but I wanted you to know why it is not. I have your book and would like to keep it. I will gladly pay for it. I hope you understand my ongoing conviction regarding this and why I have made this decision.

My pastor's letter hurt and greatly disappointed me. My church wasn't interested in my story. I responded that very afternoon, saying that I appreciated him taking time to write and explain to me about my book. I also informed him that when I'd stopped by the library this past Sunday to place a label in the book, I was told it was in the office, which I was very sorry to hear.

By publishing my story, I have laid bare my life, my thoughts, and my struggles with homosexuality. I believe God has been leading me all along to write this book so that those who continue to believe that homosexuality is something a person chooses can see how ridiculous that belief is. No one chooses to be gay. It's a struggle, many times without support of parents, siblings, society, or even church friends. In fact, the church friends usually condemn the loudest. That fact has always broken my heart and continues to do so.

Whenever Brenda and I visit a church that is open and affirming, I feel the tears coming all during the service because this is what I yearn for from my own church—for its members to simply accept me as the person I am.

One of the many letters I have received praising my book stated, "It was in some ways reassuring, in some ways shocking, and in the end heart warming." When I saw the word "shocking," I immediately wondered which part she was referring to. But as I read on, it was I who was shocked as I read, "The shocking part was that even a portion of your church was accepting. I worked during that time with several people who went to church there. I can't imagine any of them accepting it at that time."

Jesus told us in John 4:35b: "... open your eyes and look at the fields! They are ripe for harvest." And I tell you that Baptist churches (and others) have done irreparable damage to those homosexuals who are "ripe unto harvest" because a large majority of them literally hate the church. They know they didn't choose to be gay. They know how much they've fought it—and my book documents the many, many years I struggled against it ining active in the church and faithfully married isband. Instead of the church reaching out to gays, supporting them and loving them, gays have been mistreated, hated, and in many cases, exiled—actually forced to leave the church.

Having said all this, let me admit that I know you are in an untenable position in this regard. Even though we disagree on this subject, if your thinking were to somehow change, you couldn't afford to lead our church in a more realistic understanding of homosexuality without losing your job. Yet I believe my job is to remain faithful to my calling to share my story and God's greater story of His all-inclusive love.

As to believing homosexuals should remain celibate, the seventh chapter of First Corinthians talks a good bit about marriage, with Paul advocating that no one should marry. But he admits in verse seven that not everyone has the same gift of being able to go through life without marrying.

I thank you for listening to us and for taking us seriously. I realize the difficulty of this issue. But I also realize the difficulty in the 1800s of the slavery issue, especially in the South—and how churches failed miserably at that time to stand up for what was right. The churches also failed miserably on the issue of segregation. I think I've used this metaphor before—that churches should be the headlight, not the taillight. We (the churches) are again failing miserably when it comes to the subject of homosexuality.

❧ ❧ ❧ ❧ ❧

I'm almost embarrassed to admit that for many months after my book was published, I carried in a cloth bag one or more copies of my book to church, believing some church members would want to purchase a copy. How foolish.

Only a few church members bought one. One member of my Sunday-school class asked for three copies to share with her family, which made me feel wonderful, especially since she was one of the few people with whom I'd shared my manuscript. I then twisted the arm of one of Jim's good friends by sending him an e-mail suggesting he might want to see if he could find himself in the book, since I'd changed his name.

He agreed to meet me in the SteinMart parking lot one day in July, where I sold him a book. Some time later, when I was volunteering at our church's kiosk on Sunday morning, his wife walked up to me when no one else was around. She said, "I just want you to know I read your book, and I had no idea what you were going through." Tears came to her eyes. "I'm on your side!" Her words meant so much to me. To actually have a church member say that to me—the only one out of 400 to 500 members—thrilled me. A few others expressed support privately to Brenda, but none that we knew of who openly stood up for us.

A total of seven people from my church bought one or more copies, including those I've already mentioned. Continuing to yearn for opportunities to share my story, I sent letters in June 2014 to three women who head various book groups, offering to lead a discussion of it for their group. I never heard from any of them, even though I regularly saw them at church.

I probably should have given up, but I didn't. In my 2014 Christmas letter, I wrote the following description of our year's advocacy activities.

Brenda and I loaded up our little R-Pod camper for an unprecedented (for us) six-week combination book tour/speaking engagements/vacation during September and October. Brenda did a fantastic job of arranging my speaking schedule so that I was able to share my story with ten different groups in places like Lubbock, Silver City, NM, and the Arizona towns of Yuma, Tucson, Prescott, Flagstaff, and Sedona. Our speaking tour ended in Austin, where I shared my story at the regional PFLAG conference. A week later, still in Austin, I received an award from the Texas Association of Authors for my book, A Christian Coming Out: A Journal of the Darkest Period in My Life.

Out of the twenty-two people from my church who received my Christmas letter, only four of them had already purchased a copy of my book, and as far as I know, my Christmas letter brought no more sales. My church family simply was not interested in my story.

I was becoming disenchanted with the possibilities of ever being asked to share my story with members of my church family, which I had then been a part of for almost twenty-six years. Everyone was nice to us, friendly, kind. When we had taken our six-week trip in 2014, one of the members had actually called to make certain we were all right because she missed us. She sang in the choir and said she was accustomed to seeing us sitting toward the front of the sanctuary.

☙☙☙☙

On various occasions over the years Brenda and I invited members of my Sunday-school class to our home for an evening meal. The attendance was always wonderful. Our long table was full of happy women eating together and socializing.

When Brenda's dad passed away in October of 2012, our Sunday-school classes offered to prepare the meal for Brenda's extended family. We accepted their offer, and they provided a huge amount of delicious food for about fifteen people. They not only prepared this homemade meal but also came to our home and served us, then cleaned up the kitchen afterward. We had known many of these women for at least thirteen years.

I had always been quite open with my class about my sexual orientation, and on one Sunday in May 2014, when we were simply sharing what was going on in our lives, I indicated how much I would welcome an opportunity to share my story with some group within my own church, perhaps even my own Sunday-school department of fifty to sixty people. I could tell from the body language of those few in our room that this would never be possible. One member spoke up and said, "But we're nice to you, aren't we?"

I was shocked but couldn't immediately put my finger on the reason her statement had made me feel so uneasy. Later, when I shared her statement with others, they quickly explained, "It's as if that's all you deserve." Christians are supposed to be nice to everyone, especially members of their own church, their own Sunday-school class. I was a former teacher of this class. Of course they'd be nice to me. Why would they think that being nice to me was something for which they should be proud?

This incident instigated my questioning why I continued to be a member of First Baptist. Then on Sunday, January 25, 2015, the pastor mentioned in his sermon that the Bible is very clear that marriage is to be only between a man and a woman—that same-sex marriage is sinful. As I sat in the congregation listening to his words, I made a firm decision. I was through attending worship services at First Baptist. At that time, I had been a faithful, supportive member of this church for more than twenty-six years.

Some members of my Sunday-school class noticed my absence. Three members took time to call or write, telling me how much they missed me. The member who had purchased three copies of my book wrote a long letter saying all kinds of nice things to me.

I consider you one of the most intelligent, one of the smartest, one of the most level-headed women I know. And there are very few of those around any more. You have influenced me with your hard work, genuine spirit, and truthfulness. I personally can't turn my back to you because of you being gay. I see a person that I love and admire...The lifestyle you choose is your preference. We should be respectful of that. And I hope I have been. Your presence on Sunday morning adds so much to our little group.

I appreciated her letter very much, but my heart sank in her use of the word "lifestyle" and her belief that my being gay was my choice. I had hoped that anyone who read my book and who therefore had to be aware of my lifelong struggles with being gay would know that I never chose to be gay. My only choice was to be open and honest about my sexual orientation as opposed to hiding that fact until I was sixty years old.

After leaving First Baptist, Brenda and I began visiting First Presbyterian, where we were warmly welcomed. After visiting there for about a month, we were placed on their mailing list, and the first newsletter we received was addressed to **both** of us. What a change! Such a simple thing, but it said so very much. First Baptist always sent us two copies of everything—one to each of us at the same address.

Chapter Thirty-three

When my original book, *A Christian Coming Out,* was published in June of 2013, I was pulled in two different directions. I was certainly excited about having a book published, but I was also filled with trepidation because I'd made my innermost secrets known to the world. Actually, the "world" didn't bother me nearly as much as having my secrets made public to friends and family. That's the thought that filled me with fear. I wrestled with my decision of whether to publish for many years.

Did I really want to lay myself bare, to admit to embarrassing weaknesses, to publicize feelings and actions that would probably best be kept hidden? Should I really disclose my secrets in such a public manner? Yet I had craved to tell my life story for a long time because I've always thought it was unique and could serve as an invaluable testimony to others. I believed then, and continue to believe now, that the telling of my story in both written and verbal form is my reason for living, has always been just that, and that everything has simply been leading up to this purpose.

Much of my book was written in 2000, and at that time I so dreaded the thought of someone reading it that I used all kinds of passwords, just in case I were to drop over dead and someone would gain access to my computer. In other words, I wrote the book in a cocoon of fear. That was fifteen years ago. What a change. I now travel the country sharing my story with whatever group will welcome me. PFLAG groups invite me to speak, as do some churches, college classes, and others. When I speak, I simply share my story.

Because I'm now seventy-seven, I'm thankful for every opportunity to tell my story, as I know the time will come when I'll be unable to keep up with this kind of schedule. In 2013, Brenda and I traveled in North Carolina, where I spoke to eight PFLAG groups. In 2014, we traveled in New Mexico and Arizona, where I addressed ten groups. In 2015, we traveled in Florida, Alabama, and Louisiana, where I told my story to six PFLAG groups, a large social-justice group at the University of Central Florida in Orlando, four churches, plus a radio interview in New Orleans.

While in Lubbock, Texas in 2014, I had an opportunity to speak to a gathering at the Metropolitan Community Church, a church that will always be special to me. Almost fifteen years earlier, on January 16, 2000, a time immediately following my asking Jim for a divorce, when I spent several weeks in my daughter's apartment in Lubbock, I read for the first time information about Metropolitan Community Churches, churches that welcome gays. In a curious frame of mind, I'd located Laura's telephone directory to see if such a church was present in Lubbock. Much to my surprise, and delight, one was. So on Sunday morning, I dressed in a nice suit and heels, the way I normally dressed for a Sunday service, and with much trepidation as evidenced by sweaty palms and pounding heart, I drove to that church. As soon as I entered the sanctuary, I immediately knew I was way overdressed. Feeling completely out of place, I quickly and quietly slid in on the back row.

I found the worship service to be a very

emotionally moving experience because I was seeing for the first time gay couples comfortably being together in a religious setting. Tears overflowed throughout the service as gay couples behaved toward each other in the same way I was accustomed to seeing straight couples behave toward their spouses. This was a new experience for me. When Communion was offered toward the end of the service and all were invited to come to the front, I held back, unable to control my emotions. I'd never before witnessed gay couples taking communion together. I knew if I had walked to the front I would have completely broken down and cried my heart out. So I remained seated on the back row.

Returning to this church in September 2014 to share my story felt as if I had come full circle. What a milestone! And to make my visit even more memorable, a cousin who lived in a nearby town, and whom I've only seen a few times in my life, took time to come to the event and even bought a copy of my book.

That same month I was scheduled to speak in Silver City, New Mexico. As Brenda and I walked down the main street of this uniquely beautiful town, we were surprised to round a corner and see my picture on a poster advertising my upcoming presentation. Then we glanced around and saw posters advertising my talk everywhere. We must have seen twenty to thirty posters as we strolled down the main street. What a thrill!

My presentation in Silver City led to an hour-long television interview on Transition Radio, which was broadcast on the Gay Television Network. Prior to the interview in November, I went on-line to check out the station and was startled to see two large naked breasts in an advertisement. Embarrassed to think that people wanting to watch my interview would first view these breasts, I decided I couldn't proceed with the interview, feeling it was an undesirable situation in which to place myself.

I wrote the young man who'd asked me for the interview, trying to gently explain that I would have to decline his invitation. I wish I'd kept his reply, because it was very well written. He explained that as members of the LGBT community, we are constantly combating prejudice and wondered how I could explain the prejudice I was exhibiting toward the advertisement. He was right. The ad was for "falsies" for those who had undergone mastectomies, as well as for those who were transgendered. I asked forgiveness for my wrong thinking and agreed to do the interview, which turned out very well.

❧❧❧❧

Brenda and I participated in the Dallas pride parade (the Alan Ross Freedom Parade) for three or four years between 2001 and 2005, where we marched with our PFLAG group. We found the event lots of fun as well as uplifting because PFLAG always received a loud round of applause.

However, we felt uncomfortable with the dress (or lack thereof) of some of the participants. Although the parade was advertised as family friendly, we felt uncomfortable participating, concerned that our Christian example in our church might suffer due to our involvement in the pride parade. We chose to stop participating. Perhaps the conservative culture in which I was raised is reflected in both this parade participation as well as my desire to avoid seeing the falsies advertisement. A gentleman this summer presented an insight regarding outlandish dress of pride-parade participants by stating that those most outlandishly dressed are probably those crying out the loudest for help. I'll try to remember that insight.

❧❧❧❧

Life is truly amazing. I recall my mother begging me as a young girl to take a speech class. She began encouraging me when I was in high school and didn't give up even when I was in college. But I never complied. At that time, I felt I would absolutely die if I had to speak in front of a group. I recall in my high-school freshman-English class, we were required to memorize poetry and recite the poems aloud. Those of us who simply couldn't do this in front of the class were allowed to sit at the teacher's desk and recite the poem to her alone. Even then, I trembled and my hands were cold as ice. My teacher (who also happened to be my next-door neighbor) always reached over afterward to feel my cold hands because she knew how frightened I was.

When Laura was in elementary school, I worked for the Texas Beef Industry Council as their director of communications. I gradually gained self-confidence over the years as I had the opportunity to travel on my own to various cities throughout the United States speaking to numerous groups in the beef industry.

By the time this book is published, I will have shared my personal story with at least fifty-eight groups. Not only do I share my story in public, but with individuals, many who write me for help/advice. I've found others' stories to be just as unique and poignant as my own.

Because I've remained active in PFLAG ever since

Brenda and I met there in 2000, I often receive letters written to that group. In 2008, we heard from a young lesbian whose former husband had served her with a temporary restraining order and a right to modify the parent-child relationship to separate her from her young son. The husband told the court that he felt his wife and her companion couldn't adequately care for his son because they were homosexual.

This situation isn't unique in East Texas. Brenda and I wanted to help in whatever way we could, so we traveled to their hometown about an hour and a half away. We met the mother at a Starbucks, then followed her to the mediator's office, where we spent the day sitting in the lounge area simply being available if and when we were needed.

The young mother stated that the father of the child had never before shown any interest in his child, but his parents, who were wealthy and could afford a lawyer, had encouraged their son to bring suit. Their standing in the community, their wealth, and the fact that they were seeking to remove the child from its lesbian mother seemed almost too overwhelming for the mother to fight. She appreciated that we were simply present, offering emotional support, and we like to think that our presence helped her retain joint custody of her child.

※ ※ ※ ※

The letters I have received asking for advice vary from Bible Belt adults unable to come to grips with having a gay child to gays being fired because they have AIDS. Another letter was from the daughter-in-law of a closeted gay father-in-law who checked himself into a psychiatric unit, unable to face the fact that he is gay. Another came from a young gay man whose parents had attended a NARTH (The National Association for Research and Therapy of Homosexuality) convention and were promoting the value of this organization, which offers conversion therapy and other regimens they claim can change the sexual orientation of people with same-sex attraction.

A typical letter, which we received in 2009, read like this.

I have four children, and last night my sixteen-year-old daughter told me she likes girls. I've never known a gay child. Never really thought much about it and had always thought I wouldn't care if any of my children were gay. Now, I'm having difficulty digesting this news. She was crying and told me she'd been talking to one of her sisters about this for over a year! I was blown away and had no words...I sent her back to her room and told her to go back to bed. I'm sure I handled that situation wrong. But at the moment I thought that way was best. Please, if you can offer me some advice, I'd really appreciate it. I'm struggling.

I answered her with a long letter, describing the time in my life when I was the teenager in a similar situation. After sharing my story, I suggested that *she* begin another conversation with her daughter because the girl might never approach her again on this subject. I explained how children find it difficult to tell a parent he/she is gay because they want the parent to be proud of them. They've heard too many horror stories of children being disowned and kicked out of their homes when parents learn their child is gay. I predicted that once she accepted her daughter as she was and supported her through a life that will probably be difficult, she would develop an admiration for her child beyond any words she could describe today.

My replies have usually contained a portion of my personal story, along with one or both of my favorite resources. At that time, an on-line video called *Unlearning Homophobia* showed various parents talking about their gay children. (http://www.womanvision.org/straight-from-the-heart.html). I particularly like the section titled "Straight From The Heart." I've also found *A Letter to Louise* helpful. This Biblical affirmation of homosexuality can be downloaded at no charge from www.godmademegay.com.

I've been very thankful for these two excellent resources and hope they continue to help people who need them.

❧❧❧❧

I learned recently that sharing my story gives others the courage to share their own. One elderly woman was particularly moved by my account of my mother's condemnation when I was seventeen. She shared with us her personal story, which she'd never before told anyone.

She spoke of a time when she was fourteen and she and a young boy thought they'd had sex. They were both so naive and innocent they didn't know exactly what they were doing. Word somehow got back to her parents, who vociferously condemned her actions, telling her she'd ruined her life, that no decent boy would ever have anything to do with her, and that she would never be able to marry a good man because he wouldn't want her.

She internalized her parents' condemnation and predictions to such an extent she never attempted to date "a nice boy." When she was in college, she actually had sex with a "not-so-nice" fellow and realized that what she and the young boyfriend had done wasn't intercourse. Yet she continued to believe and take to heart her parents' condemnation of her actions.

Although she was friends with some really nice men who would have made good marriage material, she never dated any of them. She believed that when she told them the truth about herself, they would turn their backs to her. She ended up marrying a man she didn't particularly admire or respect. The marriage was difficult and they eventually divorced.

She told us her story to illustrate what an impact parents' words can have on young people. Her parents' shaming of her had diminished her life—and needlessly so.

॰॰॰॰॰

Along with remaining active in PFLAG and serving on their board for many years, I was also one of the first board members of Project TAG, which stands for Tyler Area Gays. In 2009 I was presented with their Advocate of the Year award. I held various offices in both these organizations, along with leading TAG's Adopt-A-Highway cleanup, their board-games group, and the ladies-dinner group.

I enjoy writing letters and occasionally have sent advocacy-type letters to our local newspaper. On July 8, 2005, one of my letters appeared in our local newspaper, informing the public of a remarkable speech that the

Spanish leader Jose Luis Rodriguez Zapetero had made when the Spanish parliament took its historic vote legalizing both gay marriage and adoption of children by gay couples. Here are some of his words.

We are enlarging the opportunity for happiness to our neighbors, our coworkers, our friends and our families: at the same time we are making a more decent society because a decent society does not humiliate its members. Today the Spanish society answers to a group of people who, during many years, have been humiliated, whose rights have been ignored, whose dignity has been offended, their identity denied and their liberty oppressed...It is true they are only a minority, but their triumph is everyone's triumph. This law will generate no evil. Its only consequence will be the avoiding of senseless suffering of decent human beings. A society that avoids senseless suffering is a better society...Today we demonstrate with this bill that societies can better themselves and can cross barriers and create tolerance by putting a stop to the unhappiness and humiliation of some of our citizens.

An individual from a nearby town wrote to me several days later, and the following statement gratified me.

If only our leader, who talks so much about freedom, was as enlightened as the leader of Spain! Thank you so much for writing to the Tyler paper, as I would not have known about the speech. It is also nice to know that there are tolerant, enlightened people like you in our midst.

The signature at the bottom of the letter was that

of a person I didn't know and have probably yet to meet.

≈≈≈≈

I've always enjoyed writing letters to the editor, about a variety of subjects. I've had letters published in our local newspaper and in *Baptists Today*, which is a news magazine of the Cooperative Baptist Fellowship. I've also been interviewed by television stations. I don't recall the subject of my first television interview, but I almost made myself sick over it. After thinking through what I wanted to say, writing it down, and memorizing it as best I could, I discovered that the reporter's questions didn't lead me into anything I'd prepared to say. I did the best I could, but I certainly wasn't proud of the results.

After that first attempt, I was called upon again and again because few people in East Texas were and are willing to speak openly for the gay population. One of my latest interviews dealt with the ruling allowing gays to participate in Boy Scouts. Because all three of my sons were Boy Scouts, because I'd served as an assistant den leader, and because I myself am gay, I was an appropriate person for that TV interview.

Then on June 26, 2015, when the U. S. Supreme Court made marriage legal for gays, Brenda and I were interviewed on our local CBS television station that morning. That afternoon, we participated in a gathering at the courthouse annex to hear our local county clerk state she would *not* be issuing marriage licenses to gays in Smith County. After her statement, a newspaper reporter began interviewing Brenda and me, while their photographer took pictures of us. The next morning our large color photo appeared top center on the front page of our local newspaper, along with an article containing our comments. I continually marvel at the changes in my life.

Two months later, I attended a League of Women Voters gathering to celebrate Women's Equality Day—a commemoration of the 1920 passage of the 19th Amendment to the Constitution, which granted women the right to vote. Several young women attended from our local newspaper. One, who happened to be an editor, kept looking at me and finally said, "I feel I've met you somewhere before."

I laughed. "You probably saw our picture on the front page of your newspaper after the Supreme Court passed the marriage amendment for gays."

I'm gradually becoming more accustomed to and at ease with my newfound notoriety.

Chapter Thirty-four

During the spring of 2015, Brenda and I contacted staff members in our city library asking permission to exhibit various PFLAG materials in one of their display cases during the month of June. We easily received that permission from a very supportive staff at the library.

During this same conversation I was asked if I would be willing to speak during a session of their Adult Summer Reading Program, developed around the theme of overcoming obstacles. I readily agreed, and the date was set for June 8. This invitation would be my first opportunity to share my story with the general public in my hometown.

On Monday, June 1, Brenda and I set up the PFLAG display. It consisted primarily of PFLAG materials. We added some colored beads and a few pins, along with several booklets, including "Safe Schools," "Guide to Being a Straight Ally," "Be Yourself," "Opening the Straight Spouse's Closet," "Guide to Being a Trans Ally," "Our Daughters and Sons," "Faith and Our Families," "Welcoming Our Trans Family and Friends," and "The Bible and Homosexuality." We also included copies of our East Texas PFLAG brochure.

Two days later, I took my seven-year-old granddaughter to the library to pick out some books and movies. When we walked in, she spotted a poster with my picture on it—advertising my upcoming talk.

"Grandmother, that's you!"

"Yes, that's me. I'll be giving a talk."

"Will they recognize you, Grandmother?"

"Yes, they'll recognize me."

As we headed for the children's area to let her choose some books, I took a quick look at the PFLAG display. It looked great, but I noticed the 20" x 12" PFLAG poster we'd attached to the adjacent brick wall had fallen down. I mentally told myself to return later and take care of that problem.

Therefore, after supper, I went to the library with some additional "sticky" to encourage that poster to stay up. When I entered the library and glanced over at the display case, I saw it was completely, totally empty. Then I looked around for the poster advertising my upcoming presentation, and it was gone. My heart sank.

I walked over to a library desk and asked what was going on. The young girl there, looking embarrassed and subdued, said, "You need to talk with the head librarian. Her office is on the third floor."

By the time I walked up the stairs, Joyce Fischer, the head librarian was waiting for me and led me into her office. "I'm just heartsick about this," she explained. "And so embarrassed." She'd received a call from the library's key leader instructing her to remove the PFLAG display and cancel my talk. City officials were concerned that it would be political simply because the library newsletter advertising my talk contained a quote from Hillary Clinton. She also explained that the concern about the display case centered around the fact that people thought it was located too close to the children's area.

"That's why we had to empty the case. We have all your materials in a box at the desk downstairs." She shook her head. "We even received a complaint here at the library. A woman called me all upset because she felt the library was promoting homosexuality. I explained to her that the library serves the entire community without regard to race, age, gender, or sexual orientation and that the library is here to promote education." Joyce said that this upset complainer had asked in a rather belligerent tone, 'Just what does the library do for Christians?'"

"Our speaker's a Christian," Joyce had stated and went on to explain that the library sets aside a special section for inspirational Christian fiction and even offers free meeting space for a regular Bible study.

"Is it a *Christian* Bible study?" the complainer had asked Joyce.

"Well, it's a *Bible* study, so I assume it's Christian. I don't know what denomination it is."

"When this complainer received no satisfaction from me," Joyce said, "she must have contacted the city manager's office. And she probably wasn't the only one."

After our visit, I picked up our box of display materials and headed home. Brenda was already aware of the problem at the library because she'd received a Facebook message from Joyce before I ever reached the library. Joyce had indicated in that message that I could speak in the library at another time, just not during the summer, when children might attend, and that the library couldn't sponsor my talk as part of a library program. The PFLAG display had to come down because it was a "political statement."

Brenda and I, especially Brenda, went into high gear, sending out e-mails informing the LGBT community of what had transpired. The news spread rapidly. Our local CBS television station interviewed us the following day, and the *Dallas Voice* talked to us by phone and wrote a wonderful article. I sent e-mails to my PFLAG list of almost 300 names, some now living in other states. Brenda posted on numerous Facebook websites. A national Gay blog (Towleroad) picked up the story. We were called for a live phone interview by KNON in Dallas for their LAMBDA Weekly segment. We asked people to contact the city manager's office and supplied the phone number, e-mail address, and snail-mail address.

That office must have been inundated with messages, because by the following afternoon, a conference call was set up between Brenda and me, the library's key leader (who is the parks and recreation director), and the assistant city manager. The city staffers contended that it was all a misunderstanding. We got everything we asked for, except the library couldn't sponsor my talk, though they could provide a room for the talk.

I personally delivered handwritten invitations to the city manager, the library's key leader, and the assistant city manager to come hear my story. Our East Texas PFLAG chapter stepped up to the plate and sponsored my presentation.

On June 8 we were grateful and humbled by the outpouring of support and attendance by the LGBT community as well as the community at large. Both the library's key leader and the assistant city manager attended. Brenda counted a total of seventy-nine present. Joyce said the library is normally thrilled to have twenty people attend an event such as this, so we ended up benefitting from all the publicity. It was a godsend.

The city manager invited Brenda and me for coffee the next week, and we chatted for almost an hour—a nice, friendly conversation. As a result, Brenda was asked if she would be willing to serve on the library programing committee. And then, when I made a second presentation in the library later that same month during a cultural-diversity meeting, the city manager himself attended.

Given the ultra-conservative Tyler culture, the city manager's office probably acquiesced to a few complaints, feared the talk would be political, and hastily pulled the PFLAG display and my talk. Brenda and I put the display case back up the day after it was taken down, but later in the month it was moved to another location on the first floor, away from the children's area.

❧ ❧ ❧ ❧

We made our third book tour during September and October 2015. By the end of this tour, I'd shared my story with groups not only in my own state of Texas, but also in North Carolina, Arkansas, Oklahoma, Louisiana, Alabama, Florida, New Mexico, and Arizona. While in Louisiana, Brenda and I had the opportunity to visit with Bob Watson, my pastor during my early coming-out years.

I was very fortunate to have had him for my pastor. Brenda and I had always considered him very welcoming and caring. When he moved on to another congregation, I told him he was simply too progressive for the conservative Baptists in East Texas.

In October, we had a delightful visit with him and his wife. We discussed stories of our travels and the current conservative political climate in Louisiana, as well as Texas. As we were saying our good-byes, he hugged me and whispered in my ear, "Thank you for your ministry."

My heart leaped at his words to realize a Baptist pastor was thanking me for sharing my coming-out story as a gay Christian.

❧ ❧ ❧ ❧

Equality for gays is progressing at a faster rate than ever before. I'm amazed at the changes occurring in my lifetime. By the time my grandchildren are grown, hopefully an overwhelming majority of the population will support gay equality.

My youngest grandchildren call me Grandmother, and Brenda, Granny. One day when my granddaughter was about four, we were in our bedroom. She looked at our bed, pointed to the left side and asked, "Grandmother, is this the side you sleep on?"

"No," Claire. "I sleep on the other side. That's where Granny sleeps."

"Oh," she said. My answer apparently satisfied her.

On another occasion, when she announced a desire to play "wedding," I replied, "Sounds like fun. Who's getting married?"

"You and Granny!"

Toward the end of 2015, when we shared with her and her mother that Brenda and I did plan to get married, my granddaughter, then seven years old, asked, "Does this mean you're going to have a baby?"

"No, we won't be having a baby," we simply said, without explaining that not only are we the same gender, but one of us is seventy-six and the other sixty-five.

❧ ❧ ❧ ❧

I spent over seventy years believing that Christians

were the good people, friends. Now I'm sorry to say that my attitude has changed. I no longer think of Christians as always being the good people. I hate to admit this, but in my mind the word Christian has become synonymous with "adversary." Whenever I hear that someone is Christian, I tighten all over, expecting something unpleasant to be said or done or thought.

ᨏᨏᨏᨏ

At long last I can honestly say, "I'm glad I'm gay." I recall attending a PFLAG meeting in which one of the women asked the group, "If there were a pill you could take that would make you straight instead of gay, would you take it?"

Several immediately replied that they certainly would. I'll never forget, though, what one member confidently stated. "No, I wouldn't. I like myself the way I am."

At that time her words shocked me. She actually liked being gay? I stared at her, trying to fathom what she meant and couldn't figure it out. Surely she wasn't serious. Who would want to be gay if you could be straight?

I spent most of my life wanting to be straight. I would have paid any amount of money to have had a pill to keep me from being gay, to make it possible for me to love a man.

But now that I have become much better acquainted with myself, with who and what God made me to be, I finally understand that woman's feelings. If someone were to ask me that same question today, I'd say, "No way would I take that pill. I like who I am."

About the Author

After spending 60 years living what most Southern Baptists would consider a "normal life" which included marrying and raising four children, Lou Anne Smoot faced a painful truth about herself--she was homosexual.

This retired public school teacher, holder of two college degrees, mother of four, grandmother of six, and Baptist Sunday School teacher, courageously changed her life in the direction she felt God was "prodding" her to go. Despite the uncomfortableness of remaining a member of her Baptist church when she divorced and began "coming out," she remained faithful to God and to her church at a time when most homosexuals her age either remained "in the closet" or turned their backs on the churches that seemed to turn their backs on them.

Lou Anne is now an activist for gay rights and was awarded the 2010 Project TAG (Tyler Area Gays) Advocate of the Year Award. She published her "brutally honest" story, *"A Christian Coming Out, A Journal of the Darkest Period in My Life"* in 2013 and has been busy speaking and sharing how God has moved in her life.